965 QUESTIONS

OF

Wole Soyinka

Questions from the Works of
Wole Soyinka

By L. Dale Richesin

Title: 965 Questions of Wole Soyinka

Description: This study will examine all of the
works of Wole Soyinka.

EAN-13:   9798672854793

Category: Nonfiction, Literary Criticism, African

Country of Publication: United States
Language: English
Search Keywords: Wole Soyinka/ African literature

Author: L. Dale Richesin

Author Biography: L. Dale Richesin is a graduate of the
University of Chicago Divinity School. He taught Old
Testament at Chicago Baptist Institute for 19 years. He has
also published *The Challenge of Liberation Theology* with
Brian Mahan (1979). Maryknoll, NY: Orbis Books and
Interpreting Disciples with Larry D. Bouchard (1983). Ft
Worth: TCU Press.

965 QUESTIONS

OF

Wole Soyinka

Questions from the Works of

Wole Soyinka

By L. Dale Richesin

Copyright 2020 by L. Dale Richesin

Published by Qoheleth Publications,
Anaktuvuk Pass, Alaska

Other Books by L. Dale Richesin
CML (950) Questions of Shakespeare
951 Questions of Bernard Shaw
956 Questions of Greek Literature
949 Questions of Moliere
952 Questions of Henrik Ibsen
953 Questions of Joyce
955 Questions of Dickens
954 Questions of George Eliot
957 Questions of Mark Twain
958 Questions of Eugene O'Neill
959 Questions of Eugene Faulkner
960 Questions of Thornton Wilder
961 Questions of Bertolt Brecht
962 Questions of Samuel Beckett
963 Questions of Harold Pinter
964 Questions of August Wilson

Forthcoming Books in the Literature Series
966 Questions of Tennessee Williams
967 Questions of Arthur Miller
968 Questions of Neil Simon
969 Questions of Edward Albee
970 Questions of Toni Morrison
971 Questions of Athol Fugard
972 Questions of Sam Shepherd
973 Questions of Alice Walker

Dedicated to my daughters:

Jennifer Romero

KeeShawn Romero

Takira Simms

965 QUESTIONS OF WOLE SOYINKA

Contents

Introduction   9

Plays
I.   A Dance of Forests   13
II.   The Swamp Dwellers   19
III.   The Strong Breed   25
IV.   The Road   31
V.   The Bacchae of Euripides   39
VI.   The Lion and the Jewel   47
VII. Kongi's Harvest   53
VIII.   The Trials of Brother Jero   59
IX.   Jero's Metamorphosis   65
X.   Madmen and Specialists   73
XI.   Death and the King's Horseman   81
XII. The Beautification of the Area Boy   89

Novels
XIII.   The Interpreters   97
XIV.   Season of Anomy   105

Memoirs
XV. The Man Died: Prison Notes   113
XVI.   Ake': The Years of Childhood   121
XVII.   Isara: A Voyage Around Essay   131
XVIII.   Ibadan: The Penkelemes Years:
A memoir 1946-1967   139
XIX.   You Must Set Forth at Dawn   147

Poetry
XX. Idanre and other poems   157
XXI.   Mandela's Earth and other poems   165

XXII.   Samarkand and Other Markets
                     I Have Known   173

    Essays
XXIII.   InterInventions: Between Defective
                     Memory and the Public Lie   183
XXIV.   Myth, Literature and the African World   187
XXV.   The Burden of Memory the Muse of
                     Forgiveness   193
XXVI.   The Open Sore of a Continent: A personal
                     Narrative of the Nigerian Crisis   197
XXVII.   Climate of Fear: The Quest for Dignity in a
                     Dehumanized World   201
XXVIII.   Of Africa   205

Bibliography   209

Introduction

Wole Soyinka. W.S. William Shakespeare. Soyinka has been called the Shakespeare of Africa. His plays, especially *Death and the King's Horsemen,* stand out with powerful characters and dramatic exchanges. But I would argue that Soyinka should be compared to Bernard Shaw. His essays argue specific political positions yet present a perspective that ages well. Soyinka's political arguments have wrestled with the British colonists, the dictators, and the generals. He was arrested, and later, fled into exile.

"For me, I respect an honest and truthful peasant more than I respect a deceitful and lying president. I was brought up to know and to believe that lying is the beginning of almost all crimes and sins. I was trained in the classic military mould as an officer and gentleman who can be taken on his word. A liar will invariably be a fraud, a rogue, a murderer." [1]

"Stirring in your yellowing scroll of ivory slogans. They scream: You'll not emboss my shroud in slogans! But if phrasemongers have indeed usurped the word, and dreams come packaged, handy like a sausage roll, the poet chooses; DANGER—DREAMS AT WORK. Now mark my slogan well." [2]

"We know. But your father drank so much, he must have drunk your share, and that of his great grandsons."[3]

---

[1] Soyinka, Wole. 2015. *InterInventions: Between Defective Memory and the Public Lie.* Ibandan: Bookcraft, p. 1.

[2] Soyinka, Wole. 1988. *Mandela's Earth and other poems.* New York: Random House, p. 56.

"In any case, the purpose is not really to indict the past, but to summon it to the attention of a suicidal, anachronistic present. To say to that mutant present: you are a child of those centuries of lies, distortion and opportunism in high places, even among the holy of holies of intellectual objectivity. But the world is growing up, while you willfully remain a child, a stubborn, self-destructive child, with certain destructive powers, but a child nevertheless. And to say to the world, to call attention to its own historic passage of lies—as yet unabandoned by some—which sustains the evil precocity of this child. Wherein then lies the surprise that we, the victims of that intellectual dishonesty of others, demand from that world that is finally coming to itself, a measure of expiation? Demand that it rescues itself, by concrete acts, from the stigma of being the wilful parent of a monstrosity, especially as that monstrous child still draws material nourishment, breath, and human recognition from the strengths and devises of that world, with an umbilical cord which stretches across oceans, even across the cosmos via so-called programmes of technological co-operation. We are saying very simply but urgently: Sever that cord. By any name, be it Total Sanction, Boycott, Disinvestment, or whatever, sever this umbilical cord and leave this monster of a birth to atrophy and die or to rebuild itself on long-denied humane foundations. Let it collapse, shorn of its external sustenance, let it collapse of its own social disequilibrium, its economic lopsidedness, its war of attrition on its most productive labour. Let it wither like an aborted foetus of the human family if it persists in smothering the minds and sinews which constitute its authentic being."[4]

---

[3] Soyinka, Wole. 1974. *The Lion and the Jewel.* New York: Oxford University Press, p. 14.

[4] Wole Soyinka. 1986. "The Past Must Address Its Present," Nobel Lecture. December 8, 1986.

Is Soyinka the next Shakespeare or the next Shaw? His excellence is most noted in the fact that I am confident that years from now someone will claim to be the next Soyinka. W.S.

Plays

I.   A Dance of Forests

1. "When you see a man hurrying, he has got" what? ("Got a load on his back. Do you think I live emptily that I will take another's cause for pay or mercy?" *A Dance of the Forests*, p. 7.)

2. "So I told her to get out. Get out and pack your things. Think of it. Think of it yourself. What did she think I was" I can't" what? ("I can't take anyone who happens to wander in, just because she claims to be my auntie." *A Dance of the Forests*, p. 9.)

3. "Unfortunately I have seen so much and I am rarely impressed by anything. But that…it was the work of" what? ("Of ten generations. I think your hands are very old. You have the fingers of the dead." *A Dance of the Forests*, p. 10.)

4. "Those obscenities again. Let us wander off by ourselves. The others can" what? ("Can deal with them." *A Dance of the Forests*, p. 11.)

5. "No, but it is dead enough here. Even my home looks dead. You see how the leaves" do what? ("Have served someone for a feast?" *A Dance of the Forests*, p. 12.)

6. "Take care of how you tempt me. I have some more questions. If you answer them sanely, you may" what? ("You may save your skin. Now which of the townspeople did you talk to?" *A Dance of the Forests*, p. 13.)

7. "He should bear no love for Eshuoro. It is not much but it is something. Let Eshuoro strip a few more dwellings naked and he won't" what? ("He won't have a friend at the welcome." *A Dance of the Forests,* p. 15.)

8. "No crime, if that's what you mean. Like your carver here, I was" what? ("I was thrown out by the nose. I know too much… about people…far too much." *A Dance of the Forests,* p. 16.)

9. "Yes, that is the name painted on it. But we prefer to call our collection, human or vehicular, by" what? ("By the names by which they are generally known." *A Dance of the Forests,* p. 17.)

10. "Now that's a blood thirsty woman. No, you cannot really punish the man. After all, how was he to foresee the consequences of" what? ("Of his actions? How was he to know that in two months from the deed, the lorry would hit another, overturn completely, and be set on fire." *A Dance of the Forests,* p. 19.)

11. "Oh no. If you think I am just pretending, go ahead and kill me right now. You'll see I don't mind at all. Of course, if I was" what? ("If I was really going to die, I would go further than that." *A Dance of the Forests,* p. 20.)

12. "I hope you like what you've started. After all you asked the question. You should" what? ("You should not complain if you get an unexpected answer." *A Dance of the Forests,* p. 21.)

13. "There is a graveyard. Find yourself a graveyard if" what? ("If you want some silence." *A Dance of the Forests*, p. 22.)

14. "I carved something to you. Of course I didn't know you. Then, I mean, I had" what? ("I had never met you. But from what I heard." *A Dance of the Forests*, p. 23.)

15. "Not to you. Not to anyone. I owe all that happened to my nature. I regret nothing. They were fools, fools to think they were" what? ("Were something better than…the other men. My other men." *A Dance of the Forests*, p. 24.)

16. "I always did want to come here. This is my home. I have always yearned to come back. Over there, nothing held me. I owned nothing, had" what? ("Had no desire to. But the dark trees and the thick earth drew me." *A Dance of the Forests*, p. 25.)

17. "He climbed higher and I pushed him down. The one who did not" what? ("Did not fall from the tree. Apprentice to my craft, till I plunged him into hell." *A Dance of the Forests*, p. 26.)

18. "Below the knee, shave and scrape him clean on the head. But thrice Oremole, slave, server to Eshuroro laughed! Let me" what? ("Let me anoint the head, and do you, my master, trim the bulge of his great. Bottom." *A Dance of the Forests*, p. 27.)

19. "Never mind. I'm only worried because he went into hiding. But I don't think he would" what? ("He would wander into the forest. I begged him not to." *A Dance of the Forests*, p. 28.)

20. "Well, believe me when I tell you that everything has misfired. These people who have come to claim our hospitality do not wish us well. We were sent by" whom? ("By the wrong people. We asked for statesmen and we were sent executioners." *A Dance of the Forests,* p. 29.)

21. "Nothing I hope. But such a lot seems to be happening. Just tell me one thing. Did I or did I not hear aright when you said" what? ("When you aid that all this was to drive off the very people we had invited to be our guests." *A Dance of the Forests,* p. 30.)

22. "Yes. It was a fine speech. But control, at some point was" what? ("Was lost to our enemies. The guests we were sent are slaves and lackeys. They have only come to undermine our strength." *A Dance of the Forests,* p. 31.)

23. "The same. And that is one descendant we overlooked. Illustrious too beyond a doubt. And they are" what? ("They are strongly linked to her. Through what crime, I do not know." *A Dance of the Forests,* p. 33)

24. "Did you think I took notice? Because it rained the day the egg was hatched the foolish chicken swore he was" what? ("He swore he was a fish. Proverb to bones and silence." *A Dance of the Forests,* p. 33.)

25. "They passed here. They stayed at this very spot and" what? ("And spoke with four people." *A Dance of the Forests,* p. 34.)

26. "If you see the banana leaf freshly fibrous like" what? ("Like a woman's breasts if you see the banana leaf shred itself, thread on thread hang wet as the crepe of grief don't say it's the wind. Leave the dead some room to dance." *A Dance of the Forests,* p. 36.)

27. "Look! It is not thunder at all. There's" what? ("There's a drunkard at the wheel." *A Dance of the Forests,* p. 38.)

28. "Fine time to tell me" what? ("To tell me he no longer needs me." What will I find at this hour but the dregs of emptied pots?" *A Dance of the Forests,* p. 40.)

29. "They were not difficult to win over. And they'll be present at the welcoming. Four hundred million of their dead will" what? ("Will crush to humans in a load of guilt. Four hundred million callously smoked to death." *A Dance of the Forests,* p. 42.)

30. "Only I may eat the leaves of the silk-cotton tree and let men cower and women run to hole. My voice is thin, my voice is shrill, my voice is" what? ("Is no child's lullaby to human ears." *A Dance of the Forests,* p. 44.)

31. "We will make use of him. If the child needs a fright then" what? The mother must summon the witch." *A Dance of the Forests,* p. 46.)

32. "I plead guilty to the possession of thought. I did not know" what? ("I did not know that it was in me to exercise it, until your Majesty's unhuman commands." *A Dance of the Forests,* p. 48.)

33. "Why do you continue this useless questioning? I have told you" what? ("I have told you that I am ready to submit my neck to..." *A Dance of the Forests*, p. 50.)

34. "I want them taken away immediately. I do not want sight or smell of them after sunset. If" what? ("If no boat can be found drown them." *A Dance of the Forests*, p. 52.)

35. "That is a fact. Mata Kharibu and all his ancestors would be" what? ("Would be proud to ride in such a boat." *A Dance of the Forests*, p. 54.)

36. "Torture! I have cause to torture you. Did you know" whom? ("The one who fell from the roof? The one who leapt to his death, on my account?" *A Dance of the Forests*, p. 56.)

37. "You must wait, like us. In any case the Forest Spirits have gone" where? ("To the gathering of the tribes. Or did you not know that—Eshuoro?" *A Dance of the Forests*, p. 59.)

38. "I take no part, but listen. If shadow, future shadows form in rain-water held in hollow leaves, this is" what? ("This is the moment for the welcome of the dead." *A Dance of the Forests*, p. 64.)

39. "Freedom indeed we have to choose our path to turn" where? ("To turn to the left or the right like the spider in the sand-pit and the great ball of eggs pressing on his back." *A Dance of the Forests*, p. 68.)

40. "Not any more. It was the same lightning that" what? ("That seared us through the head." *A Dance of the Forests,* p. 74.)

II.   The Swamp Dwellers

41. "I did not come to look for him. Came only to" what? ("To see if the rain looks like stopping." *The Swamp Dwellers*, p. 81.)

42. "I want to be here when he gives me the news. I don't want to" what? ("To fall down dead out in the open." *The Swamp Dwellers*, p. 82.)

43. "Suppose he's lost his way? Suppose he went walking in the swamps and" what? ("And couldn't find his way back?" *The Swamp Dwellers*, p. 82.)

44. "I'm going after him. I don't want to lose him too. I don't want him missing his foothold and" what? ("And vanishing without a cry, without a chance for anyone to save him." *The Swamp Dwellers*, p. 83.)

45. "If you felt for him like a true father, you'd know he was dead. But you haven't any feelings at all. Anyone would" what? ("Anyone would think they weren't your own flesh and blood." *The Swamp Dwellers*, p.84.)

46. "And the way I would go walking with you, and I could hear" what? ("I could hear their heads turning round, and one tongue hanging out and saying to the other." *The Swamp Dwellers*, p. 85.)

47. "Think hard woman. Do you not remember? We did not know" what? ("We did not know that the swamp came up as far as that part of the stream…The ground…gave…way beneath us!" *The Swamp Dwellers*, p. 86.)

48. "It ruins them. The city ruins them. What do they seek there except money? They talk to the traders, and then they" what? ("They cannot sit still...There was Gonushi's son for one...left his wife and children...not a word to anyone." *The Swamp Dwellers*, p. 87.)

49. "Most of the way wherever it was possible, I walked. But sometimes, I was forced to" what? ("To accept a lift from the ferries." *The Swamp Dwellers*, p. 88.)

50. "But you're blind. Why don't you beg like others? There is" what? ("There is no true worshipper who would deny you this charity." *The Swamp Dwellers*, p. 89.)

51. "No more, no more. All the way down the river the natives read" what? ("Read me the code of the afflicted, according to their various faiths. Some fed and clothed me." *The Swamp Dwellers*, p. 90.)

52. "Even before anyone told me, I knew exactly what I had to do to live. A staff, a bowl, and I was" what? ("I was out on the roads begging for alms from travelers, singing my prayers, pouring out blessings upon them which were not mine to give..." *The Swamp Dwellers*, p. 91.)

53. "We don't know yet. He hardly said a word to anyone before he" what? ("Before he rushed off again to see what the floods had done to his farm...The man is a fool." *The Swamp Dwellers*, p. 92.)

54. "The land that we till and live on has been ours from the beginning of time. The bounds are marked by"

what? ("By ageless iroko trees that have lived since the birth of the Serpent, since the birth of the world, since the start of time itself. What is ours is ours. But what belongs to the Serpent may never be taken away from him." *The Swamp Dwellers,* p. 93.)

55. "Did Igwezu bring a friend with him?" ("No Kadiye. This is a stranger who called at my house for charity. He is blind." *The Swamp Dwellers,* p. 94.)

56. "Here, here, take this to the drummer and stop your cackling. It will be his own fault if he doesn't come and we" what" ("We finish the lot. Pah!" *The Swamp Dwellers,* p. 95.)

57. "Yes, when the floods began and the swamps overran the land, I vowed to the Serpent that I would" what? ("That I would neither shave nor wash until the rains ceased altogether." *The Swamp Dwellers,* p. 96.)

58. Aw, shut up in a while. Igwezu himself was lucky to get her at all. He would have had to turn back" where? ("To turn back at the river if it wasn't for old Qazuri who is still ferrying travelers across the swollen stream." *The Swamp Dwellers,* p. 97.)

59. "Yes, I could feel the air growing lighter, and the clouds clearing over my head. I think" what? (I think the worse of your season is over." *The Swamp Dwellers,* p. 98.)

60. "They came in hordes, and squatted on the land. It only took an hour or two, and" what? ("And the village returned to normal." *The Swamp Dwellers,* p. 99.)

61. "I headed away from my home, and" what? ("And set my face towards the river." *The Swamp Dwellers,* p. 99.)

62. "Ay'ii the hands of the gods are" what? ("Are unequal. Their gifts become the burden of..." *The Swamp Dwellers,* p. 100.)

63. "He is not unwell. I merely asked" what? ("I merely asked him how he felt." *The Swamp Dwellers,* p. 100.)

64. "I am a wanderer, a beggar by birth and fortunes. But you own a farm. I have stood where your soil is" what? ("Is good and cleaves to the toes like the clay of bricks in the mixing; but it needs the fingers of drought whose skin is parchment." *The Swamp Dwellers,* p. 101.)

65. "Yes. Now that the rains have ceased, his vow is come to an end. He wanted me to do it, but" what? ("But I said, No, Kadiye; I am still strong and health, but my fingers shake a little now and then, and your skin is tender." *The Swamp Dwellers,* p. 101.)

66. "I am a free bondsman. I give myself willingly. I have without the asking. But I must" what? ("I must know whom I serve, for them I will not stint my labour." *The Swamp Dwellers,* p. 102.)

67. "Which death did he die—that is all I want to know. Surely a mother may say that much, and" what? ("And be forgiven the sin of lying to herself—even at the moment of the asking. And he is still my son, Igwezu he is still your own twin." The*The Swamp Dwellers,* p. 103.)

68. "Nothing but what happens to a newcomer to the race. The city reared itself in the air, and" what? ("And with the strength of its legs of brass kicked the adventurer in the small of his back." *The Swamp Dwellers,* p. 104.)

69. "The wound heals quicker if it is left unopened. What took place is" what? ("Is not worth the memory." *The Swamp Dwellers,* p. 104.)

70. "Amazing, is it not? The mothers can never be trusted…And to think" what? ("To think that she did succeed in the end!" *The Swamp Dwellers,* p. 105.)

71. "Did you make other vows, Kadiye? Were there other pleasures from which you" what? ("From which you abstained until the rains abated?" *The Swamp Dwellers,* p. 106.)

72. "No, I had my duties…People still die, you know. And" what? ("And mothers give birth to children." *The Swamp Dwellers,* p. 106.)

73. "Now what do you take us for? As if anyone in the city would" what? ("Would lend money on a farm which he had never even seen. Are they such fools— these business men of yours?" *The Swamp Dwellers,* p. 107.)

74. "Don't you want news of my wife? Have you no interest in" what? ("In the simple and unspoilt child whom you wooed on my behalf?" *The Swamp Dwellers,* p.)

75. "That was wisely spoken. You have" what? ("You have all the makings of a true bondsman." *The Swamp Dwellers,* p. 108.)

76. "And he made it clear—that the offering was from me? That I demanded the protection of the heavens on me and my house, on" what? ("On my father and my mother, on my wife, land and chattels?" *The Swamp Dwellers,* p. 109.)

77. "And when the Kadiye blessed my marriage, and tied the heaven-made knot, did he" what? ("Did he promise a long life? Did he not promise children? Did he not promise happiness?" *The Swamp Dwellers,* p. 109.)

78. "I know that the floods can come again. That the swamp will continue to laugh at our endeavours. I know" what? ("I know that we can feed the Serpent of the Swamp and kiss the Kadiye's feet—but the vapours will still rise and corrupt the tassels of the corn." *The Swamp Dwellers,* p. 110.)

79. "Is it of any earthly use to" what? ("To change one slough for another?" *The Swamp Dwellers,* p. 111.)

80. "The swallows find their next again when the cold is over. Even the bats desert dark holes in" what? ("In the trees and flap wet leaves with wings of leather." *The Swamp Dwellers,* p. 112.)

III.   The Strong Breed

81. "You will have to make up your mind soon Eman. The lorry" what? ("The lorry leaves very shortly." *The Strong Breed,* p. 115.)

82. "He comes crawling round here like" what? ("Like some horrible insect. I never want to lay my eyes on him again." *The Strong Breed,* p. 116.)

83. "He does not like farming but he knows" what? ("But he knows how to feast his dumb mouth on the fruits." *The Strong Breed,* p. 117.)

84. "Do you mean my carrier? I am unwell you know. My mother says it will" what? ("It will take away my sickness with the old year." *The Strong Breed,* p. 118.)

85. "Wait, I don't want you to spoil it. If it gets torn I shall drive you away. Now, let me see" what? ("Let me see how you are going to beat it." *The Strong Breed,* p. 119.)

86. "Because you will not listen to me. Why do you continue to stay where" what? ("Where nobody wants you?" *The Strong Breed,* p. 120.)

87. "You are wrong Sunma. I have no sense of mission. But I have found peace here and" what? ("And I am content with that." *The Strong Breed,* p. 121.)

88. "No, don't send me away. It's the least you can do for me. Let me" what? ("Let me say here until all the noise is over." *The Strong Breed,* p. 122.)

89. "Think carefully before you say any more. I am incapable of feeling indebted to you. This will" what? ("This will make no difference at all." *The Strong Breed*, p. 123.)

90. "Surely you don't want to stay indoors when" what? ("When the whole town is alive with rejoicing." *The Strong Breed*, p. 124.)

91. "I am not blind Suma. It is true I would not run away when you wanted me to, but" what? ("But that doesn't mean I do not feel things. What does tonight really mean that it makes you so helpless?" *The Strong Breed*, p. 125.)

92. "If it's the dancer I want to ask t hem to stay. At least we won't have" what? ("We won't have to miss everything." *The Strong Breed*, p. 126.)

93. "Before it's too late, let him go. For once Eman, believe what I tell you. Don't harbor him or" what? ("or you will regret it all your life." *The Strong Breed*, p. 127.)

94. "See that she gets home. I no longer trust her. If she gives trouble carry her. And see that the women" what? ("That the women stay with her until all this is over." *The Strong Breed*, p. 128.)

95. "It is a simple thing. A village which cannot" what? ("Which cannot produce its own carrier contains no men." *The Strong Breed*, p. 129.)

96. "So you've made this place. Your playground. Get away you" what? ("You untrained pigs. Get out of here." *The Strong Breed*, p. 130.)

97. "They are the ones who break first, these fools who think they were born to" what? ("To carry suffering like a hat. What are we to do now?" *The Strong Breed,* p. 131.)

98. "We must find him. It is a poor beginning for a year when our own curses remain hovering over our homes because" what? ("Because the carrier refused to take them." *The Strong Breed,* p. 132.)

99. "Omae died giving birth to your child and you think the world is ended. Eman, my pain did not begin when Omae died. Since you sent her to stay with me, son, I" what? ("I lived with the burden of knowing that this child would die bearing your son." *The Strong Breed,* p. 133.)

100.   "That I stayed at all was because of Omae. I did not expect to find her waiting. I would have taken her away, but hard as you claim to be, it would" what? ("It would have killed you. And I was a tired man. I needed peace. Because Omae was peace, I stayed. Now nothing holds me here." *The Strong Breed,* p. 134.)

101.   "Don't worry. We have him now, but things have taken a bad turn. It is no longer enough to drive him past every house. There is" what? ("There is too much contamination about already." *The Strong Breed,* p. 135.)

102.   "Are you deaf? I say I don't want to see you. Now go before" what? ("Before my tutor catches you." *The Strong Breed,* p. 136.)

103.   "None. I just wanted to see you. Do you think this place is" what? ("Is the stream where you can go and molest innocent people?" *The Strong Breed,* p. 137.)

104.   "Why? Do you really ask me why? Because you are" what? ("You are a woman and a most troublesome woman. Don't you know anything about this at all? We are not meant to see any woman. So go away before more harm is done." *The Strong Breed,* p. 137.)

105.   "Don't say anything against him or" what? ("Or I shall eat you. Isn't it you loose girls who tease him, wiggling your bottoms under his nose?" *The Strong Breed,* p. 138.)

106.   "Well! Isn't it enough that you let me set my eyes on you? Must you" what? ("Must you now totally pollute me with your touch? Don't you understand anything?" *The Strong Breed,* p. 138.)

107.   "I only want to ask one thing..." what? ("Do you promise to tell me?" *The Strong Breed,* p. 139.)

108.   "Indeed you were. Now be good enough to go into your hut until I" what? ("Until I decide your punishment. Te-he-he...now now my little daughter, you need not be afraid of me." *The Strong Breed,* p. 139.)

109.   "Good. If you will come with e now. To my hut, I shall" what? ("I shall give. You some clothes. To wash, and then we will forget all about this matter eh? Well, come on." *The Strong Breed,* p. 140.)

110.   "You are afraid of what I will say about you? Don't worry. Only if. You try to shame me, then I will speak. I am not" what? ("I am not going back to the village anyway. Just tell them I have gone, no more." *The Strong Breed*, p. 140.)

111.   "Because of that wretched man? Anyway you will" what? ("You will first talk to your father." *The Strong Breed*, p. 141.)

112.   "Don't forget all I said. I don't know how long I will be staying in my father's house as long as" what? ("As long as you remember me. When you become tired of waiting, you must do as you please." *The Strong Breed*, p. 141.)

113.   "I really came for" what? ("For a drink of water...er...is there anyone in front of the house?" *The Strong Breed*, p. 142.)

114.   "Ay, he's gone now. He is" what? ("He is a sly one, your friend. But it won't save him forever." *The Strong Breed*, p. 142.)

115.   "It is not too late. There is" what? ("There is still an hour before midnight." *The Strong Breed*, p. 143.)

116.   "I was gone twelve years but she waited. She whom I thought had too much of" what? ("Of the laughing child in her." *The Strong Breed*, p. 143.)

117.   "Any truth of that was killed in" what? (In the cruelty of her brief happiness." *The Strong Breed*, p. 144.)

118.   "He will come. All the wells are guarded. There is only" what? ("Only the stream left for him. The animal must come to drink." *The Strong Breed*, p. 144.)

119.   "I take the longer way. You know how I must do this. It is" what? ("It is quicker if you. Take the other way. Go now." *The Strong Breed*, p. 145.)

120.   "It was not only him they fled. Do you see" what? ("Do you see how unattended we are?" *The Strong Breed*, p. 146.)

IV.   The Road

121.   "Six o'clock I bet. I don't know" what? ("I don't know how it is, but no matter when I go. To sleep, I wake up when it strikes six. Now that's a miracle." *The Road,* p. 152.)

122.   "Sometimes I think, What will I do with" what? ("With all that money if I am a millionaire?" *The Road,* p. 154.)

123.   "And your driving is becoming a menace. You drivers are all the same. When you get on an endless stretch of road your buttocks open and you" what? ("You begin to fart on passengers in the first-class compartment. Is that right?" *The Road,* p. 156.)

124.   "I am so confused, but I have sight and vision only for" what? ("For the Word and it may chance, sometimes, that I miss my way among worldly humans." *The Road,* p. 158.)

125.   "Why don't you open your eyes and" what? ("And see who is now operating behind that tailboard?" *The Road,* p. 160.)

126.   "He's mad. Why you dey worry your head for dat kind person?" ("Abi you tink say Kotonu no sabbe de man dey craze." *The Road,* p. 162.)

127.   "You no fit tell me from rubble I tell you. The whole church rushed out but" what? ("But there was no need. Nobody was injured." *The Road,* p. 164.)

128.   "Did you hear what I said?" ("I hope you did because it's all true so I hope you heard every word of it. Where is Professor?" *The Road*, p. 166.)

129.   "He used to be my driver and I his tout. Now he doesn't want any part of the road—except" what? ("Except what is left of the sacrifice." *The Road*, p. 168.)

130.   "That's what would happen if your Professor came in. I don't give" what? ("I don't give a damn for that crazy guy and he know it. He's an awright guy but he sure act crazy sometimes and I'm. telling you, one of these days, he's gonna go too far." *The Road*, p. 170.)

131.   "You call it rubbish! Well you tell me why ain't I cut and bruised like all those guys? Cause timber don't turn against" what? ("Against her own son see? I'm a son of timber. And I only drive timber see." *The Road*, p. 172.)

132.   "Well he's somewhere on the road, let's go try and" what? ("And did him out." *The Road*, p. 174.)

133.   "This is what you think. But he particularly objects to stockfish. He says the smell" does what? ("Disturbs his spirits. Now go out before he comes and catches you here." *The Road*, p. 176.)

134.   "Suppose I had got killed in an accident? (It could have been us at the bridge." *The Road*, p. 178.)

135.   "Me sir! Not in the least, the thought never crossed my mind. Please Professor just" what? ("Just

forget that whole business, forget it altogether. It is just that he never wanted to drive anyway, and that's his trouble." *The Road,* p. 180.)

136.   "In the churchyard I put it in a cigarette tin and buried it near a gravestone. And swore there and then that if I uprooted it for" what? ("For any other purpose all the spirits in that burial-ground should follow me home and haunt me for three days and nights." *The Road,* p. 182.)

137.   "May your tongue of deception be rotted in pestilence from" what? ("From the enigma of the Inviolate Word." *The Road,* p. 184.)

138.   "He knows Professor will take his own time. No it's because Murano will soon arrive. That is how you will" what? ("You will become if you give up driving. You are lucky Murano doesn't know how you all depend on him." *The Road,* p. 186.)

139.   "Nearly a year since I celebrated my hundredth forgery. It is difficult to forge from scratch, and I am" what? ("I am getting old. Once I could do. Three licences in a week and not feel the strain. Now if I manage one, I feel. The life has gone from me. This needs only a little adjustment. A neat transfer, not a basic forgery." *The Road,* p. 188.)

140.   "Buried in stockfish. It was all I remembered for a long time, the smell of stockfish. Torn bodies on the road all" what? ("All smell of stockfish. Have you noticed?" *The Road,* p. 190.)

141.   "Oh I could preach them such a sermon for the occasion. I could" what? ("I could awaken pain with such memories." *The Road,* p. 192.)

142.   "Perhaps...if you promised not to look in his face...so that you could" what? ("You could not recognize him at an identification parade..." *The Road,* p. 194.)

143.   "It dragged alongside and after an eternity it pulled to the front" how? ("Swaying from side to side, pregnant with stillborns. Underline—with stillborns." *The Road,* p. 196.)

144.   "No no let them. It's much safer they all cross on foot. Get them" where? ("Get them across and I'll try and edge the lorry past the gap." *The Road,* p. 198.)

145.   "I didn't open this house for different people. And he isn't. Sooner or later you prove it like" what? ("Like flies you prove it. Like Ramadan you prove it. Like mosquito larvae on the day of the sanitary inspector you prove it. I have not worn my feet along the roads for nothing. Anyway you cannot neglect the material necessities of life. How does he intend to live since he won't drive?" *The Road,* p. 200.)

146.   "You are a very confusing person Professor. I can't follow you at all. Of course if you mean I.O.Us. then it makes" what? ("It makes some sense especially government I.O.Us. Only, will they stand up in a court of law?" *The Road,* p. 202.)

147.   "You are a strange creature my friend. You cannot read, and I presume you cannot write, but you

34

can" what? ("You can unriddle signs of the Scheme that baffle even me, whose whole life is devoted to the study of the enigmatic Word. Do you actually make this modest claim for yourself?" *The Road,* p. 204.)

148.   "Oh the Word is a terrible fire and we burned them by the ear. Only that was not the Word you see, oh no, it was not. And so for every dwelling that fell" how? ("That fell ten more rose in its place until they grew so bold that one grew here, setting its laughter against the very throat of the organ pipes." *The Road,* p. 206.)

149.   "But what was he running from? It was almost as if he was determined to die. Like" what? ("Like those willful dogs getting in the way of the wheels." *The Road,* p. 208.)

150.   "You were so determined to" what? ("To catch him you left the body!" *The Road,* p. 210.)

151.   "Charity my friend, charity. I will let you know when it is time. When a man retires he must" what? (Hye must be able to retire somewhere. I look forward to contemplation in solitude." *The Road,* p. 212.)

152.   "Sir, if I may use a little portion of your assembly time...since" when? Since our beloved Murano is not yet here sir..." *The Road,* p. 214.)

153.   "Knew him? We were at the front together. Lifelong friends me and Burma. Told him to" what? ("To come into the police force, gut oh no, he

preferred his wretched motor transport." *The Road,* p. 216.)

154.   "Sergeant Burma looked forward to retiring and doing the spare part business full-time. But of course his brakes" what? ("His brakes failed going down a hill..." *The Road,* p. 218.)

155.   "We must all stick together. Only the fallen have need of restitution. Call out the hymn. Any song will" what? ("Will do but to restore my self-confidence make it a song of praise. But mind you don't disturb me. I feel like working." *The Road,* p. 220.)

156.   "What if they were children? Is truth ever to be hidden from children? ("Yes, what thought was there was the spirit of wine upon me. It was Sunday, Palm Sunday and each child bore a cross of the tender front, yellow and green against their innocence. What I said, I did not deny." *The Road,* p. 222.)

157.   "Come on, service me the stuff. And hurry up cause like I said, we're getting out of this joint soon. I don't reckon" what? ("I don't reckon on staying long in the same place as that Professor guy." *The Road,* p. 224.)

158.   "Professor, you know I am not superstitious. I mean, in my position I can't afford to be. But this...I swear sir, I would" what? ("I would sooner you forged a hundred insurance policies." *The Road,* p. 226.)

159.   "Be even like the road itself. Flatten your bellies with the hunger of" what? ("Of an unpropitious day, power your hands with the knowledge of death." *The Road,* p. 228.)

160.   "Who meets Oro and makes no obeisance what he shall experience! When he's home he'll need" what? ("He'll need a hot massage what he shall experience." *The Road,* p. 231.)

V.   The Bacchae of Euripides

161.   "Thebes taints me with bastardy. I am turned into an alien, some foreign outgrowth of her habitual tyranny. My followers daily pay" what? ("Pay forfeit for their faith. Thebes blasphemes against me, makes a scapegoat of a god." *The Bacchae of Euripides,* p. 235.)

162.   "A scent of freedom is not easily forgotten. Have you ever slept, dreamt, and woken up with" what? ("With the air still perfumed with the fragrance of grapes?" *The Bacchae of Euripides,* p. 236.)

163.   "Generous is not the word for it. The vines went mad so to speak; they were not themselves. Something seemed to have got under the soil and" what? ("And was feeding them nectar. The weight that hung on the vines even from the scrubbiest patch. Each cluster…pendulous breasts of the wives of Kronos, bursting all over with giant nipples." *The Bacchae of Euripides,* p. 237.)

164.   "You'll get us killed. We'll be wiped out to a man. Remember" what? ("Remember the helots. Don't be rash." *The Bacchae of Euripides,* p. 238.)

165.   "Oh, but joyfully, joyfully! Welcome the new god. Joyfully sing" what? ("Sing death of the old year passing." *The Bacchae of Euripides,* p. 239.)

166.   "I don't know…why make ourselves conspicuous. Let the free citizens of Thebes declare for" what? ("Declare for this stranger or against him." *The Bacchae of Euripides,* p. 240.)

167.   "Go after them. You've been cheated of your blood this time so" what? ("So your throats are a little parched. Go up in the mountains and you'll find other juices to quench your thirst." *The Bacchae of Euripides,* p. 241.)

168.   "Kadmos was pious. Consecrating this ground in memory of my mother at least" did what? ("Kept her alive in the heart of Thebes...but that is Kadmos. Let every man's actions save or damn him. We shall see what Pentheus chooses to do." *The Bacchae of Euripides,* p. 242.)

169.   "A priest is not much use without a following, and that's soon washed away in what social currents he fails to sense or foresee. As priest and sage and prophet and I" what? ("I know not how else. I am regarded in Thebes, I must see for the blind young man who is king and even sometimes—act for him." *The Bacchae of Euripides,* p. 243.)

170.   "Something did begin. Perhaps those lashes did begin something. I feel...a small crack in" what? ("In the dead crust of the soul. Listen! Can you hear women's voices? Strange, just then I almost felt my veins race." *The Bacchae of Euripides,* p. 244.)

171.   "Yes, your son takes after. You there. But at least you don't go" where? ("You don't go at every riddle with sledgehammer and pitchfork." *The Bacchae of Euripides,* p. 245.)

172.   "And yet you ask, do we know Bromius. Who led us down from the mountains of Asia, down holy Tolus, through" what? ("Through the rugged bandit-infested hills of the Afghans, the drugged Arabian

sands, whose call have we followed through the great delta?" *The Bacchae of Euripides,* p. 246.)

173.　　　"Blessed are they who bathe in the seminal river who merge in harmony with" what? ("With earth's eternal seeding blessed they whose hands are cupped to heaven their arms shall be funnel for the rain of understanding." *The Bacchae of Euripides,* p. 247.)

174.　　　"For he is the living essence of whom, said heaven the seed is mine, this seminal germ earthed in" what? ("In sublimination of the god in flesh the flesh in god." *The Bacchae of Euripides,* p. 248.)

175.　　　"Then listen Thebes, nurse of Semele, crown your hair with ivy turn your fingers green with bryony redden" what? ("Redden your walls with berries, decked with boughs of oak and fir come dance the dance of god." *The Bacchae of Euripides,* p. 249.)

176.　　　"On the slopes where Dionysos will come run free with you in" what? ("In your labour of your dancing drudgery, your chores of dreaming—in the truth of night descends his secret—hold, embrace it." *The Bacchae of Euripides,* p. 250.)

177.　　　"He is the new life, the new breath, creative flint flood earth with his blood, let your shabby streets flow with" what? ("With his life, his light, drum him into the heart like thunder. He is the storehouse of life his bull horns empower him a bud on the autumn bough, he blossoms in you his green essence fills your womb of earth…" *The Bacchae of Euripides,* p. 251.)

41

178.   "Alright, alright. I said it was" what? ("It was a slip of tongue. Quite natural at my age." *The Bacchae of Euripides*, p. 252.)

179.   "Ah yes, look around and see if those other women dropped" what? ("Dropped bits of ivy while they were prancing about." *The Bacchae of Euripides*, p. 253.)

180.   "Here, hold on. To me. Where shall we go? Where shall we" what? ("Shall we tread this dance of life, tossing our white heads to the drums of Dionysos. Shall I lead the way to the mountains?" *The Bacchae of Euripides*, p. 254.)

181.   "I am not ashamed. Damn them, did the god declare that just the young or women must dance? They mean to" what? ("They mean to kill us off before our time." *The Bacchae of Euripides*, p. 255.)

182.   "I shall have order! Let the city know" what? ("Let the city know at once Pentheus is here to give back order and sanity." *The Bacchae of Euripides*, p. 256.)

183.   "I won't believe it. Tiresias, seer of Thebes tricked out in" what? ("In a dappled fawn-skin?" *The Bacchae of Euripides*, p. 257.)

184.   "Do not blaspheme son. Have some respect for heaven. Or at least for" what? ("At least for your elders. I am still at Kadmos, I sowed the dragon's teen and brought forth a race of supermen. You are born of earth yourself—remember that. Will the son of Ichion now disgrace his house?" *The Bacchae of Euripides*, p. 258.)

185.　　"We wash our souls, our parched and aching soul in" what? ("In streams of wine and enter sleep and oblivion. Filled with good gift Mankind forgets its grief. But wine is more!" *The Bacchae of Euripides,* p. 259.)

186.　　"Take your hands off me! Get out! Go and play" what? ("Go and play Bacchae, but don't wipe your drooling idiocy off on me." *The Bacchae of Euripides,* p. 262.)

187.　　"Shut up! I'll cut out the tongue of the next man that "what? ("That utters that name Bromius. Or Dionysos!" *The Bacchae of Euripides,* p. 265.)

188.　　"Mysteries are only for the initiates. And in this worship all, even" who? ("Even you Pentheus may enter into the Mysteries." *The Bacchae of Euripides,* p. 268.)

189.　　"I leave you now. I go, not so suffer for that cannot be. But Dionysos whose Godhead you deny will" what? ("Will call you to account. When you set chains on me, you manacle the god." *The Bacchae of Euripides,* p. 271.)

190.　　"It's happening. The palace of Pentheus totters, bulges, quivers. Rot gapes in the angry light of" what? ("Of lightning. Roots long trapped in evil crevices have burgeoned their strength empowers me, the strength of a Master…Join him! Power his will!" *The Bacchae of Euripides,* p. 274.)

191.　　"You are truly incurable. These powers that you dispute" do what? ("Move on a higher plane

43

than. Towers and city walls." *The Bacchae of Euripides,* p. 277.)

192.　"Everything—the very mountain seemed to" what? ("To sway to that one beat." *The Bacchae of Euripides,* p. 280.)

193.　"They will have a chance to surrender peacefully. If not—think who began the violence. Thebes must" what? ("Must take measures for her own safety." *The Bacchae of Euripides,* p. 283)

194.　"You found me out. I have the gift of magic, conjuring. But reality awaits you on" what? ("On the mountains. Are you still afraid?" *The Bacchae of Euripides,* p. 287.)

195.　"Look! He stands at the gate of the trap he'll find" what? ("He'll find the Bacchae and will his life he'll answer. He thrashes in the net of Dionysos, his wits are distracted. Though he fought with the will of a Titan yet, for all that, he's a man." *The Bacchae of Euripides,* p. 290.)

196.　"He's taught a new march to the household cavalry a masterpiece of precision. We'll prance through Thebes like" what? ("Like those splendid horsemen." *The Bacchae of Euripides,* p. 293.)

197.　"What is this Has this god not done enough that you still" what? ("You still call here on Bromius?" *The Bacchae of Euripides,* p. 296)

198.　"The pitiful remains lie scattered one piece among sharp rocks, others lost" where? ("Among the leaves in forest depths." *The Bacchae of Euripides,* p. 299.)

199. "Then poor woman, unshroud this great prize who the citizens of Thebes this trophy of" what? ("Of the god of joy." *The Bacchae of Euripides,* p. 302.)

200. "Can you still hear me? Do you know what I'm saying! Do you remember" what? ("Do you remember what. You said before?" *The Bacchae of Euripides,* p. 305.)

VI. The Lion and the Jewel

201.   "That is what the stewpot said to the fire. Have you" what? ("Have you no shame—at your age licking my bottom? But she was tickled just the same." *The Lion and the Jewel,* p. 3.)

202.   "Yes, and I will stand by" what? ("By every word. I spoke. But must you throw away your neck on that account? Sidi, it is so unwomanly. Only spiders carry loads the way you do." *The Lion and the Jewel,* p. 4.)

203.   "A natural feeling, arising out of envy; for, as a woman, you have" what? ("You have a smaller brain than mine." *The Lion and the Jewel,* p. 5.)

204.   "Well go there. Go to these places where women would understand you if you told them of your plans with which you oppress me daily. Do you not know what name they give you here? Have you lost" what? ("Have you lost shame completely that jeers pass you over." *The Lion and the Jewel,* p. 7.)

205.   "Now there you go again. One little thing and you must chirrup like" what? ("Like a cockatoo. You talk and talk and deafen me with words which always sound the same and make no meaning." *The Lion and the Jewel,* p. 8.)

206.   "Heaven forgive you! Do you now scorn" what? ("Do you now scorn child-bearing in a wife?" *The Lion and the Jewel,* p. 9.)

207.   "Away with you. The village says you're made, and I begin to understand I wonder that" what?

("I wonder that they let you run the school. You and your talk. You'll ruin your pupils too and then they'll utter madness just like you." *The Lion and the Jewel,* p. 10.)

208.   "The stranger. The man from the outside world. The clown who" what? ("Who fell in the river for you." *The Lion and the Jewel,* p. 11.)

209.   "Oh yes, it is. But it would have been much better for the Bale if the stranger had omitted him altogether. His image is" what? ("Is in a little corner somewhere in the book, and even that corner he shares with one of the village latrines." *The Lion and the Jewel,* p. 12.)

210.   "One leaf for" what? ("For every heart that I shall break. Beware!" *The Lion and the Jewel,* p. 13.)

211.   "We know. But your father drank so much, he must have" what? ("He must have drunk your share, and that of his great grandsons." *The Lion and the Jewel,* p. 14.)

212.   "And we are not feuding in" what? ("In something I have forgotten." *The Lion and the Jewel,* p. 16.)

213.   "What did I say? You played him to the bone, a court jester would have" what? ("Would have been the life for you, instead of school." *The Lion and the Jewel,* p. 17.)

214.   "Yes, yes…it is five full months since" what? ("Since I took a wife…five full months." *The Lion and the Jewel,* p. 18.)

215. "Fortune is with me. I was going to your house to" what? ("To see you." *The Lion and the Jewel*, p. 19.)

216. "Now that's. your other game; giving me funny names you pick up in" what? ("In your wretched books.'" *The Lion and the Jewel*, p. 20.)

217. "Sadiku, let him be. Tell your lord that. I can" what? ("I can read his mind, that I will none of him. Look—judge for yourself." *The Lion and the Jewel*, p. 21.)

218. "May Sango restore your wits. For most surely some angry god has" what? ("Has taken possession of you. Your ranting put this clean out of my head. My lord says that if you would not be his wife, would you at least come to supper at his house tonight." *The Lion and the Jewel*, p. 22.)

219. "They are lies, lies. You must not believe" what? ("You must not believe everything you hear. Sidi, would I deceive you" I swear to you..." *The Lion and the Jewel*, p. 23.)

220. "They marked the route with stakes, ate through the jungle and" what? ("And began the tracks. Trade, progress, adventure, success, civilization, fame, international conspicuousity...it was all within the grasp of Ilujinle..." *The Lion and the Jewel*, p. 24.)

221. "You are still somewhat over-gentle with the pull as if you feared to "what? ("To hurt the panther of the trees." *The Lion and the Jewel*, p. 25.)

222.　　"She will not my lord. I did my best, but she will" what? ("She will have none of you." *The Lion and the Jewel,* p. 26.)

223.　　"Did I not, at the festival of Rain, defeat the men in log-tossing match? Do I not still with" whom? ("With the most fearless ones, hunt the leopard and the boa at night and save the farmers' goats from further harm?" *The Lion and the Jewel,* p. 27.)

224.　　"I have told this to no one but you, who are my eldest, my" what? ("My most faithful wife. But if you dare parade my shame before the world..." *The Lion and the Jewel,* p. 28.)

225.　　"So we did for you too die we? We did for you in the end. Oh high and mighty lion, have we "what? ("Have we really scotched you?" *The Lion and the Jewel,* p. 30.)

226.　　"Ask no questions my girl. Just join my victory dance. Oh Sango my lord, who of us possessed" what? ("Possessed your lightning and ran like fire through that lion's tail..." *The Lion and the Jewel,* p. 31.)

227.　　"You will have to match the fox's cunning. Use your bashful looks and" what? ("And be truly repentant. Goad him my child, torment him until he weeps for shame." *The Lion and the Jewel,* p. 32.)

228.　　"Within a year or two, I swear, this town shall see" what? ("Shall see a transformation bride-price will be a thing forgotten and wives shall take their place by me." *The Lion and the Jewel,* p. 34.)

229.   "No, the madness has not gripped them—yet. Do you not" what? ("Meet with one of them?" *The Lion and the Jewel,* p. 36.)

230.   "Now that is a question which I never thought to hear except form" whom? ("From a school teacher." *The Lion and the Jewel,* p. 38.)

231.   "To strangers—no. There are tales of his open-handedness, which are never quite without a motive. But his wives report—to take one little story—how he grew the taste for ground corn and pepper—because he would not pay the price of snuff?" *The Lion and the Jewel,* p. 40.)

232.   "There are heads and skins of leopards hung around his council room. But the market is" what? ("Is also full of them." *The Lion and the Jewel,* p. 42.)

233.   "Ah! I see you love to bait your elders. One way the world remains the same, the child still thinks" what? ("Thinks she is wiser than the cotton heard of age." *The Lion and the Jewel,* p. 44.)

234.   "The work dear child, of the palace blacksmiths built in full secrecy. All is not well with it—but I will find" what? ("The cause and then Inujinle will boast its own tax on paper, made with stamps like this. For long I dreamt it and here it stands, child of my thoughts." *The Lion and the Jewel,* p. 46.)

235.   "I find my soul is sensitive, like yours. Indeed, although. There is one—no more think-one generation between yours and nine, our thoughts fly"

how? ("Fly crisply though the air and meet, purified, as one." *The Lion and the Jewel,* p. 48.)

236.   "He's killed her. I warned you. You know him, and I warned you. She's been gone" how long? ("Half the day. It will soon be daylight. And still no news. Women have disappeared before. No trace. Vanished. Now we know how." *The Lion and the Jewel,* p. 50.)

237.   "No doubt. And you are still just as slippery. I hope Baroka kills you for this. When he finds out what?" ("Finds out what your wagging tongue has done to him, I hope he beats you till you choke on your own breath..." *The Lion and the Jewel,* p. 52.)

238.   "He told me...afterwards, crowing. It was a trick. He knew Sadiku would" what? ("Would not keep it to herself, that I, or maybe other maids would hear of it and go to mock his plight." *The Lion and the Jewel,* p. 53.)

239.   "She is packing her things. She is gathering her loathes and trinkets together, and oiling herself as" what? ("As a bride does before her wedding." *The Lion and the Jewel,* p. 55.)

240.   "I invoke the fertile gods. They will stay with you. May the time come soon when you shall be" what? ("Shall be as round-belied as a full moon in a lpw sky." *The Lion and the Jewel,* p. 57.)

VII.   Kongi's Harvest

241.   "The pot that will eat fat its bottom must be" what? ("Must be scorched the squirrel that will long crack nuts its footpad must be sore." *Kongi's Harvest,* p. 61.)

242.   "This cannot continue. I shall insist that the Secretary put you all" where? ("In different sections of the camp. This cannot go on." *Kongi's Harvest,* p. 63.)

243.   "Only a foolish child lets a father prostrate to him. I don't ask to become a leper or a lunatic. I have" what? ("I have no wish to live on sour berries." *Kongi's Harvest,* p. 65)

244.   "I saw a strange sight in the market this day the day of the feast of Agemo the sun was" what? ("Was high and the king's umbrella beneath it." *Kongi's Harvest,* p. 67.)

245.   "This is the last our feet shall touch together we thought the tune obeyed us to" what? ("To the soul but the drums are newly shaped and stiff arms strain on stubborn crooks, so delve with the left foot for ill-luck; with the left again for ill-luck." *Kongi's Harvest,* p. 69.)

246.   "The subject is an image of the Reformed Aweri Fraternity of which you are" what? ("Of which you are a member in your waking moments." *Kongi's Harvest,* p. 71.)

247. "Don't waste my time with" what? ("With apologies. You know who I am of course." *Kongi's Harvest*, p. 73.)

248. "Because I warn you, I'm" what? ("I'm a very dangerous man. I don't care what her reputation is, mine is also something to reckon with." *Kongi's Harvest*, p. 75.)

249. "I am being practical. Now let us see the problem as part of" what? ("Part of a normal historic pattern. This means in effect that—Kongi must prevail." *Kongi's Harvest*, p. 77.)

250. "Not me. Didn't you hear what I said? Came out, just like" what? ("Just like that, spontaneous." *Kongi's Harvest*, p. 79.)

251. "Kongi says, the period of isolated saw and wisdoms is over, superseded by" what? ("By a more systematic formulation of comprehensive philosophies—our function, for the benefit of those who still do not know it." *Kongi's Harvest*, p. 81.)

252. "I know, I know. You wait until" when? ("Until we all break the fast on that New Yam." *Kongi's Harvest*, p. 83.)

253. "You would appear to be something of one yourself. No, to tell you the truth, my interest has" what? ("Has been purely clinical." *Kongi's Harvest*, p. 85.)

254. "Oh no, we were very thorough. Make no mistake about that, we picked" what? ("The kind of

men for the job who would be thorough." *Kongi's Harvest,* p. 87.)

255.　　"If she is who I'm sure now she is, this should" what? ("This should interest her." *Kongi's Harvest,* p. 89.)

256.　　"Hm. I think I'll t rust your judgement. Tell them they can begin work on" what? ("On my next book as soon as the new one is released." *Kongi's Harvest,* p. 91.)

257.　　"Oh, I leave that to you. Release" whom? ("Release all those who have served their court sentences." *Kongi's Harvest,* p. 93.)

258.　　"The enactment of it alone should appeal to him. Kabiyesi loves to act roles like Kingship. For him, Kingship is" what? ("Is a role." *Kongi's Harvest,* p. 95.)

259.　　"I feel like dancing naked. If I could again believe" what? ("Believe I would say it was a sign from heaven." *Kongi's Harvest,* p. 97.)

260.　　"You shouldn't worry about my women. They" what? ("They accepted it long ago." *Kongi's Harvest,* p. 99.)

261.　　"The ostrich also sports plumes but I've yet to see" what? ("That wise bird leave the ground." *Kongi's Harvest,* p. 101.)

262.　　"I should have believed it. I was warned you might go" where? ("You might go back on your word." *Kongi's Harvest,* p. 103.)

263.   "All this is quite unnecessary Kabiyesi. We appreciate your zeal and I assure you it will" what? ("It will go unmentioned. But it is your presence our Leader requires." *Kongi's Harvest,* p. 105.)

264.   "I will have to leave you. The other Obas are already arriving. Someone has to be" where? ("To be there to group each entourage in their place." *Kongi's Harvest,* p. 107.)

265.   "GO and tell. That to the Leader's men. Their yam is pounded, not with the pestle but with" what? ("But with stamp and a pad of violet ink and their arms make omelet of stubborn heads, via police trunchions." *Kongi's Harvest,* p. 109.)

266.   "No. Your son has his senses intact. He must" what? ("He must know what he is doing." *Kongi's Harvest,* p. 111.)

267.   "It means nothing. Nothing can alter what today will bring. And your compliance is" what? ("Is a vital part of it." *Kongi's Harvest,* p. 113.)

268.   "Well, I will not bear the offering past" what? ("Past the entrance to the mosque only a phony drapes himself in deeper indigo than the son of the deceased." *Kongi's Harvest,* p. 115.)

269.   "We must be aware of spies. I've put him through the standard tests. He's no" what? ("No fifth columnist." *Kongi's Harvest,* p. 117.)

270.   "I should have come to the same training school as you. Now tell me, what are the realities of

conflict as" what? ("As propounded by your royal sage?" *Kongi's Harvest,* p. 119.)

271.   "They should have been here to cheer in my men. We intend to" what? ("To lodge a vigorous complaint." *Kongi's Harvest,* p. 121.)

272.   "Kabiyesi! I had begun to rack my brain for some excuse I hadn't used before to" what? ("To explain your absence." *Kongi's Harvest,* p. 123.)

273.   "Yes, but I stopped them at the gate which is exactly where they will be left until the very end. At the gate is where we" what? ("Where we promised we would welcome them." *Kongi's Harvest,* p. 125.)

274.   "An important man will swear he feels the pangs of labour; when the maniac finally looks over the wall, he finds that there, agony is" what? ("Agony is the raw commodity which he has spent lives to invent." *Kongi's Harvest,* p. 127.)

275.   "I could do nothing to stop him. When he heard that the reprieve had been withdrawn…there was" what? ("There was simply nothing I could do. He said he had to do it and no one else." *Kongi's Harvest,* p. 129.)

276.   "Good friend, how far is it to the border? What! Well, well, if it isn't" what? ("If it isn't my bold lion of Isma." *Kongi's Harvest,* p. 131)

277.   "The man is a philosopher. We have exchanged many areas of wisdom. Right now he is" what? ("He is my travelling companion." *Kongi's Harvest,* p. 135.)

278.   "Good luck sir. I shall precede you on active service, non-stop until I am safe" where? ("Beyond the frontier. On what of this failed carpenter? Shall I take him with me—that is, if you don't mind?" *Kongi's Harvest,* p. 137.)

279.   "Don't pound the king's yam in a small mortar small las the spice is it cannot be" what? ("It cannot be swallowed whole. A shilling's vegetable must appease a halfpenny spice." *Kongi's Harvest,* p. 139.)

280.   "Now for this second coming is time for harvest this second coming is for" what? (Is for pounding of yams the mortar spills over." *Kongi's Harvest,* p. 141.)

VIII. The Trials of Brother Jero

281.   "I am a Prophet. A prophet by birth and by inclination. You have probably seen" what? ("Seen many of us on the streets, many with their own churches, many inland, many on the coast, many leading processions, many looking for processions to lead, many curing the deaf, many raising the dead." *The Trials of Brother Jero,* p. 145.)

282.   "I suppose we all do our best, but after all these years one would think" what? (One would think you could set me down a little more gently." *The Trials of Brother Jero,* p. 147.)

283.   "You've forgotten the mat. I know it's not much, but I would like something to sleep on. There are women who sleep in" what? ("In beds of course, but I'm not complaining. They are just lucky with their husbands, and we can't all be lucky I suppose." *The Trials of Brother Jero,* p. 149.)

284.   "Yes, thanks be to God. I—er—I hope you have not come to" what? ("To stand in the way of me and my work." *The Trials of Brother Jero,* p. 150.)

285.   "It is early in the morning. I am not going to let you infect my luck with" what? ("With your foul tongue by answering you back. And just you keep your cursed fingers from my goods because that is where you'll meet with the father of all devils if you don't" *The Trials of Brother Jero,* p. 151.)

286.   "Help! Thief! Thief! You bearded rogue. Call yourself" what? ("A prophet? But you'll find it easier

to get out than to get in." *The Trials of Brother Jero,* p. 151.)

287.   "I don't know what the world is coming to. A thief of a Prophet, a swindler of a fish-seller and" what? ("And now that thing with lice on his head comes begging for money. He and the Prophet ought to get together with the fish-seller their mother." *The Trials of Brother Jero,* p. 152.)

288.   "She passes here every morning, on her way to" what? ("To take a swim. Dirty-looking thing!" *The Trials of Brother Jero,* p. 153.)

289.   "Pray with me, brother. Pray with me. Pray for me against" what? ("Against this one weakness…against this one weakness, O Lord." *The Trials of Brother Jero,* p. 154.)

290.   "A-ah, you have troubles and you could not" what? ("You could not wait to get them to God. We shall pray together." *The Trials of Brother Jero,* p. 154.)

291.   "Apostate. Have I not told you the will of God in. this matter? But I've got to beat her, Prophet. You must" what? ("You must save me from madness." *The Trials of Brother Jero,* p. 155.)

292.   "Forgive this sinner, Father. Forgive him by day, forgive him by night, forgive him" when? ("In the morning, forgive him at noon." *The Trials of Brother Jero,* p. 156.)

293.   "They begin to arrive. As usual in the same order. This one who always come earliest, I have

prophesied that he will" what? ("He will be made a chief in his home town. That is a very safe prophecy. As safe as our most popular prophecy, that a man will live to be eighty if it doesn't come true." *The Trials of Brother Jero,* p. 157.)

294.   "Rise, brother Chyme. Rise and let the Lord enter into you. Apprentice of the Lord, are you not he upon" what? ("Upon whose shoulders my mantle must descend?" *The Trials of Brother Jero,* p. 157.)

295.   "Then why do you harden your heart? The Lord says that you may not beat" what? ("The good woman whom he has chosen to be your wife, to be your cross in your period of trial, and will you disobey him?" *The Trials of Brother Jero,* pp. 157-158.)

296.   "What did you do to her? ("Nothing I was only drumming and then she said I was using it to abuse her father." *The Trials of Brother Jero,* p. 158.)

297.   "You haven't blessed" what? ("The water, Brother Jeroboam." *The Trials of Brother Jero,* p. 159.)

298.   "Father forgive her. Amen. Father forgive me. Amen. Make you" what? ("Make you forgive me. Father. Amen." *The Trials of Brother Jero,* p. 159.)

299.   "Yes, Father, make you forgive us all. Make you save us from" what? ("From palaver. Save us from trouble at home. Tell our wives not to give us trouble." *The Trials of Brother Jero,* p. 160.)

300. "For God's sake I beg you...I was not abusing your father. I was only" what? ("I was only drumming...I swear to God I was only drumming..." *The Trials of Brother Jero*, pp. 160-161.)

301. "Prayers late afternoon as always. Brother Jeroboam says God" does what? ("God keep you till them. Are you all right, Brother Jero?" *The Trials of Brother Jero*, p. 161.)

302. "No, no. I was only thinking how little women have changed since" when? ("Since Eve, since Delilah since Jezebel. But we must be strong of heart." *The Trials of Brother Jero*, p. 162.)

303. "Remember, it must be done in your own house. Never show the discord within your family to the world. Take her" where? ("Take her home and beat her." *The Trials of Brother Jero*, p. 162.)

304. "The Son of God appeared to me again this morning robed just as he was when he named you my successor. And he placed his burning sword on" what? ("On my shoulder and called me his knight. He gave me a new title---but you must tell it to no one—yet." *The Trials of Brother Jero*, p. 163.)

305. "I do my share as I've always done. I cooked" what? ("I cooked you your meal. But when I ask you to bring me some clean water, you forget." *The Trials of Brother Jero*, p. 163.)

306. "I thought you were a bit early to get back. You haven't been" where? ("You haven't been to work at all. You've been drinking all day." *The Trials of Brother Jero*, p. 164.)

307.   "I hope you have ropes to tie me on the bicycle, because I don't" what? ("I don't intend to leave this place unless I am carried out. One pound eight shillings is no child's play. And it is my money not yours." *The Trials of Brother Jero,* p. 164.)

308.   "Shut your big mouth before I shut it for you. And you'd better start to" what? ("to watch your step from now on. My period of abstinence is over. My cross has been lifted off my shoulders by the Prophet." *The Trials of Brother Jero,* p. 165.)

309.   "I won't get on that thing unless" what? ("Unless you kill me first." *The Trials of Brother Jero,* p. 165.)

310.   "Brother Jeroboam, curse this man for me. You may keep the velvet cape if you" what? *f you curse this foolish man. I forgive you your debt. Go on, foolish man, kill me. If you don't kill me you don't do well in life." *The Trials of Brother Jero,* p. 166.)

311.   "I'm not touching you but I will if you" what? ("If you don't answer my question." *The Trials of Brother Jero,* p. 166.)

312.   "So…so…Suddenly he decides I may" what? ("I may beat my wife, eh?" *The Trials of Brother Jero,* p. 167.)

313.   "Then you ought to let the Prophet see to him. I had a brother once who had? What? ("Who had the fits and foamed at the mouth every other week. But the Prophet cured him. Drove the devils out of him, he died." *The Trials of Brother Jero,* p. 167.)

314.	"I could teach him a trick or two about" what? ("About speech-making. He's a member of the Federal House, a back-bencher but with one eye on a ministerial post." *The Trials of Brother Jero,* p. 168.)

315.	"Indeed the matter is quite plain. You are not of the Lord. And yet such is" what? ("Is the mystery of God's ways that his favour has lighted upon you… Minister…Minister by the grace of God." *The Trials of Brother Jero,* p. 168.)

316.	"Yes, brother, we have met. I saw this country plunged into strife. I saw" what? ("I saw the mustering of men, gathered in the name of peace through strength." *The Trials of Brother Jero,* p. 169.)

317.	"What for…why, why, why, why 'e do am? For two years 'e no let me" what? ("No let me beat that woman." *The Trials of Brother Jero,* p. 169.)

318.	"No, it is not possible. I no believe that. If no so, how they come quarrel then. Why she go sit. To" what? ("For front of 'in house demand all 'in money. I not eat am yet…" *The Trials of Brother Jero,* p. 170.)

319.	"Protect him therefore. Protect him when he must lead this country as" what? ("As his great ancestors have done." *The Trials of Brother Jero,* p. 170.)

320.	"He is falling asleep. When I appear again to him he'll think I have" what? ("I have just fallen from the sky." *The Trials of Brother Jero,* p. 171.)

IX. Jero's Metamorphosis

321.   "In time of trouble it behoves us to come together, to forget old enmities and" what? ("And bury the hatchet in the head of a common enemy…no, better take that out. It sounds a little unchristian wouldn't you say?" *Jero's Metamorphosis,* p. 175.)

322.   "You are indeed kind, Sister Rebecca. I don't know what I would" what? ("I don't know what I would do without you." *Jero's Metamorphosis,* p. 176.)

323.   "Has earth anything to offer the true Christian, Brother Jero? How often have you" what? ("How often have you said yourself." *Jero's Metamorphosis,* p. 177.)

324.   "Bailiffs like all simmers are welcome in my church, Brother Ananaias. But I do not" what? ("I do not welcome them in my humble abode." *Jero's Metamorphosis,* p. 178.)

325.   "All right, then. I came to tell you you're going to need all that cunning of yours very soon. The City Council have" what? ("Have taken a final decision. They're going to chuck us out. Every last hypocritical son of the devil." *Jero's Metamorphosis,* p. 179.)

326.   "Now, or I'll go in that room and tell whoever is there you were" what? ("You were hiding and spying on them. I'll shout and tell them you're right there." *Jero's Metamorphosis,* p. 180.)

327.   "You are known to be a violent man. The Prosecutor can make it robbery with" what? ("With violence. And you know what that means." *Jero's Metamorphosis*, p. 181.)

328.   "Kindly stop arguing with me. It is not in my character to" what? ("To skulk and hide until a mere charlatan is out of the way. I prefer to confront him squarely even if he's the devil himself." *Jero's Metamorphosis*, p. 182.)

329.   "Hell is true sir. I was living hell but" what? ("But did not know it until Brother Jero pointed the path of God to me." *Jero's Metamorphosis*, p. 183.)

330.   "Of course it's a bloody waste. Eighty words per minute and a hundred and twenty shorthand. You had enough will-power to resist" what? ("The revolting advances of a lecherous Chief Eviction Officer on the rampage, you are trusted sufficiently to be assigned an official duty which is most essential to our national economy and what happens—you permit yourself to be bamboozled by a fake prophet, a transparent charlatan..." *Jero's Metamorphosis*, p. 184.)

331.   "Shameless sinners who acquire wealth from the misfortunes of others? Will you make money off" what? ("Off sin and iniquity." *Jero's Metamorphosis*, p. 185.)

332.   "Save this sinner, Lord, save this sinner. Protect her from bribery oh Lord. Protect her from corruption!" *Jero's Metamorphosis*, p. 186.)

333.   "Good day, Corporal Chummy. I'm afraid the Captain could not come today, but I will" what? ("I will do my humble best to deputize for him." *Jero's Metamorphosis,* p. 187.)

334.   "It is much better for man to have only one teacher. I begin to get used to Captain Winston and" what? ("And then somebody else comes. Captain Winston understands how to teach me." *Jero's Metamorphosis,* p. 188.)

335.   "I no talk so? You done come with your t trouble. I say I go wait for Captain Winston you say you go fit teach me. Now you come dey bother me with" what? ("With music notation. Na proper man dey. Take. Traumpet play abi na music?" a*Jero's Metamorphosis,* p. 189.)

336.   "And now we shall begin all over again. We will forget all about" what? ("All about this for the moment shall we? Captain Winston said. That. You were a natural on the trumpet and I suppose he is right." *Jero's Metamorphosis,* p. 190.)

337.   "What! You no know wetin pepper be? Captain Winston, as soon as I say" what? ("I say pepper 'e know wetin I mean one time." *Jero's Metamorphosis,* p. 191.)

338.   "It's no ghost, brother Chume. It is no apparition that stands before you. Assure yourself that you are well again and suffer" what? ("Summer no more from hallucinations. It is I, your old beloved master the Prophet Jeroboam. Immaculate Jero, Articulate Hero of Christ's Crusade." *Jero's Metamorphosis,* p. 192.)

339.   "If to say I get my cutlass inside your head that time this world for done become" what? ("Become better place. They can hang me but. I for become saint and martyr. I for die de whole world go call me Saint Chume." *Jero's Metamorphosis,* p. 193.)

340.   "What man, be he so swift of foot can run unaided upon a sandy shore? Could you think to escape" what? ("The hounds of God's judgement and the law?" *Jero's Metamorphosis,* p. 194.)

341.   "I had my doubts for a while but I should have known better. These Salvation my brothers may be" what? ("May be washed in the red blood of the Lord, but the black blood of the Bar Beach brotherhood proves stronger every time." *Jero's Metamorphosis,* p. 195.)

342.   "The trumpet of the Lord, Chume! It sounds the clarion to duty. There is a time for" what? ("For everything, so says the Lord." *Jero's Metamorphosis,* p. 196.)

343.   "I am only the instrument of the Lord's will. Now get up and" what? ("And let's go. The others are awaiting and we have much to do." *Jero's Metamorphosis,* p. 197.)

344.   "No, we take our leave. For the third time tonight we have been insulted by" what? ("By a common riff-raff of the calling. We take our leave." *Jero's Metamorphosis,* p. 198.)

345.   "Trust me. I know what. I am doing Sister. More drinks for our brothers. Fill up" what? ("Fill up

the cups Sister Rebecca." *Jero's Metamorphosis*, p. 199.)

346.   "And now, dear brother shepherds of the flock, let us" what? ("Let us waste no more time." *Jero's Metamorphosis*, p. 200.)

347.   "Read this, Brother Matthew. These are" what? ("These are the minutes of the meeting of Cabinet at which certain decisions were taken." *Jero's Metamorphosis*, p. 201.)

348.   "Patience Brothers, patience. 'It is proposed however, that since the purpose of public execution is for" what? ("For the moral edification and spiritual upliftment of the people, one respectable religious denomination be licensed to operate on the Bar Beach." *Jero's Metamorphosis*, p. 202.)

349.   "What does Jeroboam have in mind, exactly? You didn't call us together without" what? ("Without some idea in your head." *Jero's Metamorphosis*, p. 202.)

350.   "And dangerous. Very dangerous. I refuse to remain one moment longer if such remarks are permitted. We are" what? ("We are not here to look for trouble. I dissociate myself from that remark." *Jero's Metamorphosis*, p. 203.)

351.   "They have already. The seed was well planted and it has taken root. Tomorrow the Tourist Board shall" what? ("Shall propose a certain religious body for the new amphitheatre." *Jero's Metamorphosis*, p. 204.)

352.   "Precisely against what? ("We don't know anymore than our secular models. They await a miracle, we will" what? ("We will provide it." *Jero's Metamorphosis,* p. 205.)

353.   "Christ! Those fat pockets begging to be picked while their owners are" what? ("Are laughing at the poor devil at the stake. It's a sin to be missing from this garden of Eden." *Jero's Metamorphosis,* p. 206.)

354.   "I'll stick out for Colonel. I may be slightly, see what I mean, but I know what's what? I'm" what? ("An educated man and that's a rare commodity in this outfit. Present company naturally excepted, General." *Jero's Metamorphosis,* p. 207.)

355.   "It is our hope that you have come here to put an end to" what? ("To the schemes of this rapacious trader on piety who calls himself." *Jero's Metamorphosis,* p. 208.)

356.   "We on this side place our trust in your integrity not to "what? ("To accede to any such request." *Jero's Metamorphosis,* p. 209.)

357.   "We are already in business. Of course we expect you to declare that all land actually occupied as of now by the various religious bodies would" what? ("Would from now on be held in trust, managed and developed by the newly approved representative body of all apostolic bodies." *Jero's Metamorphosis,* p. 210.)

358.   "Please give me the credit of having done my homework. You forget we have had" what? ("We

have had a formidable ally in the person of Colonel Rebecca, your former Confidential Secretary." *Jero's Metamorphosis*, p. 211.)

359.   "When Joshua blows the trumpet, kt will be your duty to" do what? ("To make the miracle happen. The walls shall come tumbling down or you will have some explaining to do." *Jero's Metamorphosis*, p. 212.)

360.   "After all, it is the fashion these days to" what? ("To be a desk General." *Jero's Metamorphosis*, p. 213.)

X.   Madmen and Specialists

361.   "Sure it does. If it's the right one he can take it out now. The left is" what? ("The left is my evil eye and I need it a while longer." *Madmen and Specialists,* p. 217.)

362.   "What congregation, woman? Who said I was ever a preacher? You were never anything. Go and find" what? And find some decent work to do." *Madmen and Specialists,* p. 218)

363.   "It is your neighborhood, you say, Si Bero. What are you doing to" what? ("To drive people away?" *Madmen and Specialists,* p. 219.)

364.   "In a way you may call us vultures. We clean up the mess made by others. The populace should be" what? ("Should be grateful for our presence. If there is anyone here who does not approve us, just say so and we quit." *Madmen and Specialists,* p. 220.)

365.   "That woman's herbs are not just herbs. She hoards them and treats them like children. The whole house is full of twigs. If it's a straightforward business, why doesn't she use them" Or" what? ("Or sell them or something." *Madmen and Specialists,* p. 221.)

366.   "One thing I disapproved of in the Old Man was" what? ("He didn't discriminate. Talk of casting pearls before swine. Vendetta my foot." *Madmen and Specialists,* p. 222.)

367.   "Think not that I hurt you but that truth hurts. We are" what? ("We are all seekers after truth. I am

a specialist in truth." *Madmen and Specialists,* p. 223.)

368.   "You have touched it with a…" what? ("With a fine needle, fine, fine needle." *Madmen and Specialists,* p. 224.)

369.   "Beginning to worry like every foolish woman. He'll come back. He and his father. There is" what? ("There is too much binds them down here." *Madmen and Specialists,* p. 226.)

370.   "So here we are, Si Bero. Bring out the herbs and" what? ("And let us catch the smell of something in your kitchen while we are about it." *Madmen and Specialists,* p. 227.)

371.   "Your mother is in a bad mood not me. Not get working instead of" what? ("Instead of dragging yourself in people's way. Get busy. You know how I like them sorted out." *Madmen and Specialists,* p. 228.)

372.   "No. I'm quite good at it, actually. One stroke and" what? ("And clean. Through the tendons. Bang through the ball-and-socket, believe me. I never touch the marrow." *Madmen and Specialists,* p. 229.)

373.   "Last night when we got him into that underground place she was fast asleep. We didn't" what? ("We didn't make a noise." *Madmen and Specialists,* p. 231.)

374.   "You can't tell me to get out. We teamed together without your help and" what? ("And we are

not doing badly as it is. You can't come here and break us up." *Madmen and Specialists,* p. 232.)

375.　　"That should remind you I do know how to slap people around. And you'd better remember "what? ("Remember some other things I know. You weren't just discharged because of your—sickness. Just remember that…and other things." *Madmen and Specialists,* p. 233.)

376.　　"Bare feet, wet earth. We've wetted your good earth with" what? ("With something more potent than that, you know." *Madmen and Specialists,* p. 234.)

377.　　"I hope it's a good seed. That was two lives we poured into her hands. Two long lives spent" what? ("Spent pecking at secrets grain by grain." *Madmen and Specialists,* p. 235.)

378.　　"None other, sister, none other. The Big Braids agreed I was" what? ("I was born into it. Not that that was any recommendation. They are all submental apes." *Madmen and Specialists,* p. 237.)

379.　　"Not quite the same think young lady, not quite the same thing. The doctor used to" what? ("Used to make those extracts with his own hand." *Madmen and Specialists,* p. 238.)

380.　　"Had only one letter from him all that time. Told me he was doing recuperative work among" whom? ("Among some disabled fellows. No forwarding address, if you please. I couldn't even continue our old debate by post." *Madmen and Specialists,* p. 239.)

381.   "Out of your world, little sister, out of your little world. Stay in it and" what? ("And do only what I tell you. That way you'll be safe." *Madmen and Specialists,* p. 241.)

382.   "It's not his charitable propensities I am concerned with. Father's assignment was" what? ("Was to help the wounded readjust to the pieces and remnants of their bodies." *Madmen and Specialists,* p. 242.)

383.   "You can see me, he said, you can see me. Look at. Me with your mind. I swear I began to" what? ("To see him. Then I knew I was insane." *Madmen and Specialists,* p. 243.)

384.   "Where the cycle is complete will as be found. As of the beginning, we" what? ("We praise thee." *Madmen and Specialists,* p. 244.)

385.   "For your Divinity to have control, the flock must be without control. Epilepsy seems to be the commonest for—at least, I have" what? ("I have witnessed much that is similar." *Madmen and Specialists,* p. 246.)

386.   "It's all very well for you to talk. You could get around even then. I sometimes think God made" what? ("God made you out of rubber or something." *Madmen and Specialists,* p. 247.)

387.   "Can't you guess what it is by" what? ("buy where he scratches himself at night?" *Madmen and Specialists,* p. 248.)

388.   "Yes, more or less the same words. But just as I want to get up, I" what? ("I wake up from the blasted dream!" *Madmen and Specialists,* p. 249.)

389.   "I don't know anything. You on the contrary appear to know everything. Isn't that right? You" what? ("You know everything." *Madmen and Specialists,* p. 251.)

390.   "You would, wouldn't you? You would try that on me. Me! Shall I teach you what to say? Choie! Particularity! What redundant self-deceptive notions! More? More? Insistence on" what? ("On a floppy old coat, a rickety old chair, a moth-eaten hat which no certified lunatic would ever consider wearing, a car which breaks down twenty times in twenty minutes, an old idea riddled with the pellets of incidence." *Madmen and Specialists,* p. 252.)

391.   "Oh yes, there is. I am the last proof of the human in you. The last shadow. Shadows are tough things to" what? ("To be rid of. How does one prove he was never born of man? Of course you could kill me…" *Madmen and Specialists,* p. 253.)

392.   "Your faces, gentlemen, your faces. You should see your faces. And your mouths are" what? ("And your mouths are hanging open." *Madmen and Specialists,* p. 254.)

393.   "Perhaps you heard my spasms tuning up. It's like a set of wires Old Man. Something touches them, they hum, and" what? ("And off I go." *Madmen and Specialists,* p. 256.)

394.   "A man like me is letting himself down to say he is surprised by anything, but…I was surprised at you, Old Man. You may say I was" what? ("I was a bit let down. We may be on opposite sides of the camp, but I like to see a man stand up for himself." *Madmen and Specialists,* p. 257.)

395.   "Hey, remember the song the Old Man wrote to celebrate the occasion? Visit of the First Lady to" where? ("To the Home for the de-balled." *Madmen and Specialists,* p. 258.)

396.   "You heard wrong. I am giving you warning to clear out of here. Pick up" what? ("Pick up your lice and rags and get out." *Madmen and Specialists,* p. 259.)

397.   "In ancient Athens they didn't just have a quorum. Everybody was" where? ("Everybody was there! That, children, was democracy." *Madmen and Specialists,* p. 261.)

398.   "To me you are simply another organism, another mould or strain under the lens. Sometimes a strain proves" what? ("Proves malignant and it becomes dangerous to continue with it. In such a case there is only one thing to do." *Madmen and Specialists,* p. 262.)

399.   "You've used it before, haven't you? Or something similar. I saw" what? ("I saw your victims afterwards." *Madmen and Specialists,* p. 263.)

400.   "She's a good woman and her heart is strong. And it is that kind who tire suddenly in their sleep and" what? ("And pass on to join their ancestors.

What happens then?" *Madmen and Specialists,* p. 268.)

XI.   Death and the King's Horseman

401.   "When the horse sniffs the stable does he not strain at the bridle? The market is the long-suffering home of" what? ("Of my spirit and the women are packing up to go." *Death and the King's Horseman,* p. 9.)

402.   "Far be it for me to belittle the dwellers of that place but, a man is either born to his art or he isn't. And I don't know" what? ("I don't know for certain that you'll meet my father, so who is going to sing these deeds in accents that will pierce the deafness of the ancient ones." *Death and the King's Horseman,* p. 10.)

403.   "There is only one home to the life of a river-mussel; there's only one home to" what? ("To the life of a tortoise; there is only one shell to the soul of man; there is only one world to the spirit of our race." *Death and the King's Horseman,* p. 11.)

404.   "And take my good kinsman Ifawomi. His hands were like" what? ("His hands were like a carver's, strong and true. I saw them tremble like wet wings of a fowl one day he cast his time-smoothed opal across the divination board." *Death and the King's Horseman,* p. 12.)

405.   "There was fear in the forest too. Not-I was lately heard even in the lair of beasts. The hyena cackled lout Not-I, the civet twitched his fiery tail and" what? ("And glared: Not-I." *Death and the King's Horseman,* p. 13.)

406.　　"That rock which turns its open lodes into the path of lightning. A gay thoroughbred whose stride" does" what? ("Disdains to falter though an adder reared suddenly in his path." *Death and the King's Horseman*, p. 14.)

407.　　"The world was mine. Our joint hands raised houseposts of trust that withstood the siege of envy and" what? ("And the termites of time. But the twilight hour brings bats and rodents-shall I yield them cause to foul the rafters?" *Death and the King's Horseman*, p. 15.)

408.　　"You who are breath and giver of my being how shall I" what? ("How shall I dare refuse you forgiveness even if the offence were real." *Death and the King's Horseman*, p. 16.)

409.　　"For a while we truly feared our hands had" what? ("Our hands. Had wrenched the world adrift in emptiness." *Death and the King's Horseman*, p. 17.)

410.　　"I embrace it. And let me tell you, women— I like this farewell that" what? ("That the world designed, unless my eyes deceive me, unless we are already parted, the world and I, and all that breeds desire is lodged among our tireless ancestors." *Death and the King's Horseman*, p. 18.)

411.　　"Enough, enough, you all have cause to know me well. But, if you say this earth is" what? ("Is still the same as gave birth to those sons, tell me who was that goddess through whose lips I saw the ivory pebbles of Oya's reiver-bed." *Death and the King's Horseman*, p. 19.)

412.　　"Who speaks of pleasure? O women, listen! Pleasure palls. Our acts should have" what? ("Should have meaning. The sap of the plantain never dries." *Death and the King's Horseman*, p. 20.)

413.　　"Only the curses of the departed are to be feared. The claims of one whose foot is" where? ("On the threshold of their abode surpasses even the claims of blood." *Death and the King's Horseman*, p. 21.)

414.　　"The living must eat and drink. When the moment comes, don't" what? ("Don't turn the food to rodents' droppings in their mouth." *Death and the King's Horseman*, p. 22.)

415.　　"I said nothing. Now we must go prepare your bridal chamber. Then these same hands will" what? ("Will lay your shrouds." *Death and the King's Horseman*, p. 23.)

416.　　"Nonsense, He's a Moslem. Come on Amusa, you don't believe in all this nonsense, do you? I thought you were" what? ("I thought you were a good Moslem." *Death and the King's Horseman*, p. 24.)

417.　　"Darling, why are you getting rattled? I was only trying to be intelligent. It seems hardly fair" to what? ("Just to lock up a man—and a chief at that—simply on the er…what is that legal word again?" *Death and the King's Horseman*, p. 26.)

418.　　"No master. He will not kill anybody and no one will kill him. He will" what? ("He will simply die." *Death and the King's Horseman*, p. 27.)

419.   "Don't you remember? He's that chief with whom I had" what? ("With whom I had a scrap sone three or four years ago. I helped his son g et to medical school in England, remember? He fought tooth and nail to prevent it." *Death and the King's Horseman,* p. 28.)

420.   "No, I don't think he knew. At least he gave no indication. But you couldn't really tell with him. He was" what? ("He was rather close you know, quite unlike most of them. Didn't give much away, not even to me." *Death and the King's Horseman,* p. 29.)

421.   "What do you mean you don't know? It's only two years since" what? ("Since your conversion. Don't tell me all that holy water nonsense also wiped out your tribal memory." *Death and the King's Horseman,* p. 30.)

422.   "I know you better than that Simon. You are going to have to do something to stop it—after you've" what? ("After you've finished blustering." *Death and the King's Horseman,* p. 31.)

423.   "Who the hell gives a damn! I had a sudden vision of our Very Reverend Macfarlane drafting another letter of" what? ("Another letter of complaint to the Resident about my unchristian language towards his parishioners." *Death and the King's Horseman,* p. 32.)

424.   "Oh, I don't know. As a coat-of-arms perhaps. Anyway it won't be" what? ("It won't be anything to touch this." *Death and the King's Horseman,* p. 33.)

425.   "Official business you white man's eunuch? Official business is taking place where you want to go and it's a business you" what? ("You wouldn't understand." *Death and the King's Horseman,* p. 34.)

426.   "Madam Iyaloja, I glad you come. You know me. I now like trouble but duty is duty. I am here to arrest" whom? ("To arrest Elisein for criminal intent. Tell these women to stop obstructing me in the performance of my duty." *Death and the King's Horseman,* p. 36.)

427.   "How do you find the place? The natives are alright. Friendly? Traceable. Not a teeny-weeny" what? ("Restless? Well. A teeny-weeny bit restless. One might even say, difficult." *Death and the King's Horseman,* p. 38.)

428.   "Oh you mothers of beautiful brides! (The dancing stops. They turn and see him, and the object in his hands. Iyaloja approaches and" what? ("And gently takes the cloth from him." *Death and the King's Horseman,* p. 40.)

429.   "I know the wickedness of men. If there is weight on the loose end of your sash, such weight as no mere man can shift; if your sash is earthed by" what? ("By evil minds who mean to part us at the last..." *Death and the King's Horseman,* p. 42.)

430.   "Elsesin Alafin, I no longer sense your flesh. The drums are changing now but you have g one far ahead of the world. It is" what? ("It is not yet noon in heaven, let those who claim it is begin their journey home. So why must you rush like an impatient bride: why do you race to desert your

Oluhun-iyo?" *Death and the King's Horseman,* p. 44.)

431.   "Some strange custom. They have sir. It seems because the King is dead some important chief has to" what? ("Has to commit suicide." *Death and the King's Horseman,* p. 46.)

432.   "Yes yes yes of course. Come on man, speak up. Hey, didn't we give them some colourful fez hats with" what? ("With all those wavy. Things, yes, pink tassels…" *Death and the King's Horseman,* p. 48.)

433.   "Let's look at you. What a fine young man you've become. Grand but solemn. Good God, when did you return? Simon never" what? ("Never said a word. But you do look well Olunde. Really!" *Death and the King's Horseman,* p. 50.)

434.   "For you. For your people. And to think he didn't even know you were coming back! But how do you happen to be here? Only this evening we were" what? ("We were talking about you. We thought you were still four thousand miles away." *Death and the King's Horseman,* p. 52.)

435.   "That a disaster beyond human reckoning be spoken of as a triumph? No. I mean, is there no mourning in the home of the bereaved that such blasphemy is" what? ("Is permitted?" *Death and the King's Horseman,* p. 54.)

436.   "But you explained it yourself. My medical training perhaps. I have seen death too often. And the soldiers who returned from" where? ("From. The

front, they died on our hands all the time." *Death and the King's Horseman,* p. 56.)

437.	"Yes. Just a minute. There are armed policemen that way and they have" what? ("They have instructions to let no one pass. I suggest you wait a little. I'll er…yes, I'll give you an escort." *Death and the King's Horseman,* p. 58.)

438.	"Leave me alone! Is it not enough that you have" what? ("That you have covered me in shame! White man, take your hand from my body!" *Death and the King's Horseman,* p. 60.)

439.	And not merely my life but the lives of many. The end of the night's work is not over. Neither this year nor the next will see it. If I wish you well, I would pray" what? ("I would pray that you do not stay long enough on our land to see the disaster you have brought upon us." *Death and the King's Horseman,* p. 62.)

440.	"I warned you, if you must leave a seed behind, be sure it is not tainted with the curses of" what? ("Of the world. Who are you to open a new life when you dared not open the door to a new existence? I say who are you. To make so bold?" *Death and the King's Horseman,* p. 67.)

XII.   The Beautification of the Area Boy

441.   "It's a good display, not so? And to. think all I did was" what? ("Was breathe against the horizon." *The Beautification of the Area Boy,* p. 5.)

442.   "You mustn't tire. Never give up. You apply the first time, they turn you down you" what? ("You try and try again. I was rejected six times you know. When I was like you, on the receiving end." *The Beautification of the Area Boy,* p. 6.)

443.   "No. Today I start on a different journey. I begin the long journey to the kingdom of lost souls. I shall" what? ("I shall relieve them of their torment." *The Beautification of the Area Boy,* p. 7.)

444.   "It is the kind of day when unbelievers are shamed and the faithful exalted. Look at that horizon—there, where" what? ("Where the sun is just rising. Have you ever seen a dawn the likes of that?" *The Beautification of the Area Boy,* p. 8.)

445.   "You'll never know what. It is to wake into day on the rooftops—yes, those rooftops you call dirty—to wake up on the skyline face to face with" what? ("With every day a different face of itself, just as your mind has painted it before you fell asleep." *The Beautification of the Area Boy,* p. 9.)

446.   "Doing what. I have finally accepted I was meant for. My head is clear on that score. As clear as that sky you see" what? ("You see blossoming before my presence…yes, my journey to the kingdom of souls begins today." *The Beautification of the Area Boy,* p. 10.)

447.   "But you are early. None of your people ever gets here until" when? ("Until at least. Thirty minutes after I've set up for business." *The Beautification of the Area Boy,* p. 11.)

448.   "Judge say na in dey make the climate now. De say "what? ("Na in dey tell the sky what to do. De man done craze patapata." *The Beautification of the Area Boy,* p. 12)

449.   "Appearances are deceptive. There may be a method in his madness—that's what" who says? ("That's what William Shakespeare says on the subject." *The Beautification of the Area Boy,* p. 13.)

450.   "You are the original doubting Thomas. But these things happen, that's" what? ("That's all I can tell you. You see all. those corpses with their vital organs missing—breasts in the case of women, the entire region of the vagina neatly scooped out." *The Beautification of the Area Boy,* p. 14.)

451.   "As you see me, Bro, as you see me. Five naira eva no fit fill picken belle these days, how much more" what? ("How much more grown man like me?" *The Beautification of the Area Boy,* p. 15.)

452.   "My voice needs lubricating. So bring that other stuff you keep for" whom? ("For special customers. Give me one shot with the change." *The Beautification of the Area Boy,* p. 16.)

453.   "No blame me, blame Oga Sanda, na in teach me all the bad songs. Anyway, wait small. I nearly reach" what? ("I nearly reach the part wey celebrate

the Civil War wey drive you commot for Ikot Ekpenbe." *The Beautification of the Area Boy,* p. 17.)

454.   "The other day, I lie for my bed and the radio suggest say I sick for" what? ("For my head cause the government say me get no option but to wage war against corruption I pinch myself to be sure I awake." *The Beautification of the Area Boy,* p.)

455.   "If I thought they could, I wouldn't be out here every morning sweating over these pots to pay for your school fees. And anyway, who was" what? ("Who was talking to you?" *The Beautification of the Area Boy,* p. 19.)

456.   "You'll never get over that war. Not ever. Nobody does. It would be abnormal. But you must forget" what? ("You must forget the fish-ponds, Mama. And the orange groves." *The Beautification of the Area Boy,* p. 21.)

457.   "Don't mind him. Hye thinks people aren't wise to their tricks. I no longer park where vandals and" what? ("And extortionists like him operate," *The Beautification of the Area Boy,* p. 22.)

458.   "If there's one think I hate, it's" what? ("It's disloyalty. People should be loyal." *The Beautification of the Area Boy,* p. 23.)

459.   "The pilot charge him double after he see all dat super fancy interior. In fact, I remember, he even wan' cancel" what? ("He wan' cancel his safe conduct altogether." *The Beautification of the Area Boy,* p. 24.)

460.　　"Seven months and seven days he spent with them. T Hey landed the saucer in his front garden you know. All silver and blue, about" what? ("About the size of a football field." *The Beautification of the Area Boy,* p. 26.)

461.　　"You wait small. As our people say, na cudgel go teach creman sense; na hunger go reform labourer picken wey dream say in papa be" what? ("Be millionaire." *The Beautification of the Area Boy,* p. 27.)

462.　　"No mind me, I beg. Na this sight of your bicycle come begin remind me. Sai! Dat time, money dey walka street and buka, supermarket and" what? ("And corner shop like 'e no get tomorrow." *The Beautification of the Area Boy,* p. 28.)

463.　　"Come on my friend. I can see say you no sabbe trade at all. Taiwanese no dey bring tires here, na only" what? ("Only motor spare part." *The Beautification of the Area Boy,* p. 29.)

464.　　"I heard. The more reason to knock her out with a brand-new haircut. Don't worry, I don't waste time. And it's" what? ("It's fifty per cent discount since you are my first customer." *The Beautification of the Area Boy,* p. 31.)

465.　　"All the street mongrels are going to snap at your heels, you'll see. Area Boy on bicycle! The police will" what? ("Will use it as an excuse to lock you up, mark my words. Mr Sanda, you'd better get ready to go and bail him." *The Beautification of the Area Boy,* p. 32.)

466.   "No not that kind of choking. I can't really describe it. As if" what? ("As if someone was vomiting and cursing at the same time." *The Beautification of the Area Boy,* p. 36.)

467.   "Now, now, that's not the way to speak to our foreign guests. The man has had" what? ("The man has had a bad experience, and it should make us feel ashamed." *The Beautification of the Area Boy,* p. 40.)

468.   "Yes, yes, it's something I've noticed myself. For someone doing" what? ("Doing security job, you seem very well educated." *The Beautification of the Area Boy,* p. 44.)

469.   "Don't try to be funny. I'm looking at you helping big men and their women with "what? ("With their shopping bags, holding open their car doors while they roll in their fat bodies, and there you are funny, ludicrous." *The Beautification of the Area Boy,* p. 48.)

470.   "AIDS! The whole world has gone made. I tell you I'm just" what? ("I'm just a victim of vanishing organs. My genitals have disappeared— what has that to do with AIDS?" *The Beautification of the Area Boy,* p. 52.)

471.   "It's a military government, isn't it? That means they can" what? ("They can defy even God's commandments." *The Beautification of the Area Boy,* p. 56.)

472.   "Oh yes. That dream of mine, I suppose. Dreams make me nervous, that's true. But the grief belonged to "whom? ("To someone else. I was

smothered by its approach, but the grief was elsewhere. Are you hungry?" *The Beautification of the Area Boy,* p. 60.)

473.　"You will be proud to remember this moment, my friend. You have all, in many ways, contributed to" what? ("To this last act of my transfiguration." *The Beautification of the Area Boy,* p. 64.)

474.　"The conga law of equity yields economic parity. You squeeze the left and" what? ("And waste its resources on the right. Cast a little to the Left etc." *The Beautification of the Area Boy,* p. 68.)

475.　"Any time I encounter the rodents in open air, like today, I let them" what? ("I let them nibble at the loaf of liberation." *The Beautification of the Area Boy,* p. 72.)

476.　"Then tell me what is that procession passing through? What force was it that expelled them? Is this" what? ("Is this a sight one encounters in peace time?" *The Beautification of the Area Boy,* p. 76.)

477.　"They've had masses of warning under the civilian regime, even some feeble, half-hearted eviction attempts. But the law courts" what? ("Always interfered." *The Beautification of the Area Boy,* p. 80.)

478.　"I don't just want the traffic to be stopped. I am not interested in" what? ("I am not interested in the usual road blocks. I want this sector sealed up entirely." *The Beautification of the Area Boy,* p. 84.)

479.   "That's not a knife, you blind recruit. That's a bayonet. I told you she's an army wife. How else do you. Think she would be" what? ("How else do you think she would be in possession of a bayonet? She has a gun too, you're lucky she chose not to use it." *The Beautification of the Area Boy,* p. 88.)

480.   "This is obviously a highly sophisticated gathering, which is" what? ("Which is only to be expected. And now…please put your hands together for the bridegroom." *The Beautification of the Area Boy,* p. 92.)

Novels

XIII. The Interpreters

481.　　"Metal on concrete jars by drink lobes. This was Sagoe, grumbling as he" what? ("As he stuck fingers in his ears against the mad screech of iron tables." *The Interpreters,* p. 7.)

482.　　"That kind of power would only be a hobby. And there is plenty of it as these tempters from home always impress on me. Oh there is power, all right. Either way, ally with the new gods or" what? (Or hold then to ransom." *The Interpreters,* p. 13.)

483.　　"The fish began a little amphibious game thrashing wildly and darting suddenly behind a rock. to" what? ("To stare at some unseen pursuer." *The Interpreters,* p. 19.)

484.　　"From side to side Sekoni shook his head with increasing violence and Bandele said quietly, 'Now you've gone and made it worse.' They waiting a few more seconds for it and" what? ("And Sekoni erupted at last with P-p-p-profanity!" *The Interpreters,* p. 25.)

485.　　"Surprisingly, he had allowed the police to lead him off without resistance. There was another Commission of Enquiry, but" what? ("By. Then Sekoni lay in a mental hospital." *The Interpreters,* p. 31.)

486.　　"The mother braced herself for battle. This was the whole point now, the entire point of the midnight visit. 'He didn't say, but people have been'" what? ("'Have been telling me that you are going with a Northerner.'" *The Interpreters,* p. 37.)

487.   "I wouldn't pay much attention, Koa continued. You get these spiteful types everywhere and" what? ("And those ones were—and a doleful shake of the head—anyway I don't need to tell you. You know how catty people can be." *The Interpreters,* p. 43.)

488.   "She looked at him then with wonder and" what? ("And he grew uncomfortable." *The Interpreters,* p. 49.)

489.   "Egbo had sat down; anxiously he felt in his pockets and" what? ("And was reassured by the thickness of his wad. A small boy came up, a small sharp face with generous cicatrix." *The Interpreters,* p. 55.)

490.   "It was the maddest morning to pick for riling the girl, but Sagoe had" what? ("Had only encountered the wardrobe—he had never been in the bedroom before—and had been senseless through Dehinwa's trial with aunt and mother." *The Interpreters,* p. 61.)

491.   "Her reaction amazed him because almost immediately tears came to her eyes. To hide them she began searching the room again, with" what? ("With a ferocity she did not formerly display." *The Interpreters,* p. 67.)

492.   "They both jumped as. The hum of machines was harshly supplemented by" what? ("By a sudden

H-r-r-r, and a strangulated sound froze Sagoe to the spot." *The Interpreters,* p. 73.)

493.   "Sagoe was silent. No need to be modest, I am sure you consider yourself" what? ("An intelligent man." *The Interpreters,* p. 79.)

494.   "This time Sagoe was so intent on the man's face that he saw the schnapps signal. The green waistcoated waiter" did what? ("Appeared also to know his man, reacting almost before Winsala raised his face in the expert tilt." *The Interpreters,* p. 85.)

495.   "Chief Winsala, his huge frame shrunken, his confidence collapsed, waited in deep fog, resigned to" what? ("To the beginning of a shameful scheme, degrading to a man of his position." *The Interpreters,* p. 91.)

496.   "It was gratifying to sow the seeds of Voidancy on the continent of Europe, but" what? ("But in a way, it was a small defeat, for I was powerless against their damned regression..." *The Interpreters,* p. 97.)

497.   "And now Sir Derin was dead. Sagoe felt for strength in his legs, wondering why he felt" what? ("Why he felt compelled to go and see him buried." *The Interpreters,* p. 103.)

498.   "The man sopped, a jelly now, and convinced also. That he had" what? ("He had lost hope of a pardon by his delay in obeying the officer. He prostrated right inside the car, wringing his hands for pity." *The Interpreters,* p. 109.)

499.   "By some strange, imprecise, unthinking agreement the fleeing youth could be" what? ("Could be killed. The carelessness angered Sagoe, but it excited him also." *The Interpreters,* p. 115.)

500.   "Impatient now, Egbo cried 'Is it so impossible to seal off the past and" what? ("And let it alone?" *The Interpreters,* p. 121.)

501.   "Till he grew bold with fear, and angry, truly angry. What mean trick was this? Whose was the dark-sheltered laughter spying on his plight? And his anger mounted, seeing" what? ("Seeing only the blackmail of fear." *The Interpreters,* p. 127.)

502.   "They walked then towards the river, waded through the rockpools" where? ("To a smooth porpoise back which was Egbo's favourite bed." *The Interpreters,* p. 133.)

503.   "The drive was choked with cars at the big party and Sagoe said" what? ("Let's return the car and walk back." *The Interpreters,* p. 139.)

504.   "Sweat had broken free on the neck of a husband. Nothing kept him earthed but the desperate wish that the floor might" what? ("Might open and swallow him. His motions became palsied and his palms clammed on a cigarette until it snubbed out." *The Interpreters,* p. 145.)

505.   "He walked rapidly, half-expected some form of pursuit but unable to tell why. A neighbouring dog began to" what? ("Began to bark and he stopped." *The Interpreters,* p. 151.)

506.   "The man had recovered and was his street-neon pallor again. He sat like" what? ("Like a drowned cadaver, sitting bent as if he would quarrel with gravity." *The Interpreters*, p. 158.)

507.   "'My name is Lazarus,' said the man in lace-fringed robes, all white. 'My name is Lazarus, not'" what? ("'Not Christ, Son of God.'" *The Interpreters*, p. 164.)

508.   "And in his name, unto the service of the Lord our God, I ask" what? (I ask you to receive our brother Apostle, a sinner who is born again, a sinner who is washed in the blood of Christ and has chosen the path of righteousness." *The Interpreters*, p. 171.)

509.   "Why don't you go ahead and paint him, Kola? Then I would" what? ("I would use the painting in my feature, give it some kind of dimension...I don't know how exactly, the idea is just winging its way into my brain." *The Interpreters*, p. 178.)

510.   "Sorry, didn't catch what you said. Sagoe made no reply, and began to wonder if" what? ("If the risk of Peter wasn't preferable to this. You know, the stranger said, I find you fellows a most unfriendly bunch in this country." *The Interpreters*, p. 184.)

511.   "I prefer my own company. Stay up here and write. I am writing my second book, a historical novel set in Africa. And then, with" what? ("With a mad edge to his voice, you are not listening." *The Interpreters*, p. 190.)

512.   "Good. And there are no mosquitoes at all. Too high, I imagine. I'll sleep here and" what? ("And can use the bedroom." *The Interpreters,* p. 197.)

513.

The face of the campus had changed, the sounds were different, the movement, within it more ordered—almost in set sequences as" what? ("As one conference group filtered from one hall to the other and back to the gross dormitories, now sadly depopulated." *The Interpreters,* p. 203.)

514.   "Monica began to pull her. That's enough now, mother. I think he has" what? ("He has learnt his lesson, haven't you Kola?" *The Interpreters,* p. 210.)

515.   "But Kola had seen Joe as he came past the block, and Joe was" what? ("Was then fully dressed, standing in the balcony." *The Interpreters,* p. 217.)

516.   "A change in the wind, bringing the acrid smell of petrol and the sight of a barrel on its side told the rest. There was no other human within sight, and now he" what? ("He made out the two figures who waited at the other end of the trap, Lazarus and Noah." *The Interpreters,* p. 223.)

517.   "Some minutes later, recovering his calm, he said, I must try and see" what? ("Try and see that Noah does not return to the gutter." *The Interpreters,* p. 230.)

518.   "Bandele came out of the car, and Egbo leapt out suddenly away from the physical intimacy of

him" where? ("Alone in a car with Joe Golder, and followed them." *The Interpreters,* p. 237.)

519.   "They were getting late for the recital and they knew it, but none of the rose to suggest" what? ("To suggest that they leave." *The Interpreters,* p. 243.)

520.   "End of interval; and the bell recalled them, distant and shrill like" what? ("Like a leper's peal. But they stood unbelieving." *The Interpreters,* p. 251.)

XIV. Season of Anomy

521.   "A quaint anomaly, had long governed and"
what? ("And policed itself, was so singly-knit that it
obtained a tax assessment for the whole populace and
paid it before the departure of the pith-helmeted
assessor, in cash, held all property in common."
Season of Anomy, p. 2.)

522.   "The old man spoke with the pride of one
who had witnessed the moment of triumph, the glitter
in his eyes was" what? ("Was not the borrowed flame
of the historian." *Season of Anomy,* p. 10.)

523.   "The old man sprinted out to meet him as he"
what? ("As he beached the Corporation motor-boat
and helped out Iriyise." *Season of Anomy,* p. 18.)

524.   "In the middle of the night Ofeyi started out
of sleep, an inspired certainty rendered the prospect
of" what? ("Of sleep futile for the rest of the night."
Season of Anomy, p. 26.)

525.   "Stumped, the Chairman scratched his head.
In spite of serious tutoring packed with samples by
his I.Q.—the Intellectual Quota on the Directors'
Board—until he grew confident in" what? ("In his
own ability to spot the most. Subtly disguised insult
or subversiveness in the campaign lyrics, a phrase or
two did manage to stump him." *Season of Anomy,* p.
34.)

526.   "Nothing, nothing. His manner became
decisive. Go and get ready. Tonight you will do"
what? ("Tonight you will do the Pandora's Box. Go

105

and tell Zaccheus and then vanish into the crowd."
Season of Anomy, p. 42.)

527.   "I humbly beg to remind you that this is"
what? ("This is a matter of concern to me as Head of
the Corp. responsible for the day-to-day admin. of
etc. etc." *Season of Anomy*, p. 30.)

528.   "I knew we had chosen the right man for the
job and you can ask anyone on this table and" what?
("And he will tell you the same." *Season of Anomy*,
p. 58.)

529.   "Those roadside queens of the petty trade,
ethereal in the morning light before" what? ("Before
the earthy transformation for their confrontation with
bargaining humanity." *Season of Anomy*, p. 66.)

530.   "I ain't telling. Seems to be about
somebody's mother. He's flying man, flying.
Handed me" what? ("Handed me a song yesterday
and I've been trying out a few arrangements." *Season
of Anomy*, p. 74.)

531.   "Conjurer, incantatory words floated through
Ofeyi's lips. He got up from the bed at last" and
what? ("Wrapping the bed sheet around him and
walked towards her." *Season of Anomy*, p. 82.)

532.   "Skirting the edge he sleep-walked to where
the canoe lay, pushed the sheath of pitch and" what?
("And corkwood onto the pool and sat on its cross-
bench." *Season of Anomy*, p. 90.)

533.   "She came forward and took his hand. But
you still don't believe it was fated. You think it is"

what? ("It is all an accident, my brother a doctor in your country, our plane cancelled on my way to visit him, and just you and I in that lounge." *Season of Anomy,* p. 98.)

534. "He kept his eyes on the prow-riven sea, refused to acknowledge the lithe old man who had" what? ("Who had leapt out from the meeting-house at the should and raced to the shore, only to be confronted by the receding churn of water." *Season of Anomy,* p. 106.)

535. "But only because it brings me a feeling of euphoria, why I don't know. The flux of" what? ("The flux of dust and light I suppose when it isn't actually in your eyes, the that is, I get s tings and prickles all over my skin. My body becomes pounds lighter." *Season of Anomy,* p. 114.)

536. "So when these blaspheming strangers came you thought Allah had smiled on you? They were visitors sent from" where? ("From heaven to make your fortune?" *Season of Anomy,* p. 122.)

537. "When ledgers were questioned which could not be explained even in terms of the ever accommodating roads and projects that defied penetration, curfew town absorbed" what? ("Absorbed the mission millions into its benevolent purity and experimental essence." *Season of Anomy,* p. 130.)

538. "Not far away, rehearsals for the big parade continued. The quarterly meeting of the Cartel would be" what? ("Would be incomplete without

full-dress airing of the props of power." *Season of Anomy,* p. 138.)

539.   "This intimate corruption of their power loomed larger in the scale of menace than" what? ("Than the catalogue of brazen thievery and daylight massacres." *Season of Anomy,* p. 146.)

540.   "They split his family open before his eyes then dragged him live through the streets" how? ("Tied him to their land rover." *Season of Anomy,* p. 154.)

541.   "The tableau held some moments longer. The two travelers had become part of I t, immobilized by the strangeness of the sight, expectant also, wondering" what? ("Wondering what was the meaning of the hunters' silent attitude. Ofeyi wondered if their car had been observed by the hunting group." *Season of Anomy,* p. 162.)

542.   "Don't worry. I don't take foolish risks. Before you made your way back I had already worked it out. If you hadn't showed up I was" what? ("I was going to come anyway, taking a driver with huge tribal marks." *Season of Anomy,* p. 170.)

543.   "He swung the car back on to the main road and brought it to the outer iron gates. Before they reached the sentinel box he could. See" what? ("He could see the gateman already speaking into a telephone." *Season of Anomy,* p. 178.)

544.   "She ignored him, went straight to the father. 'Dad, I hope you haven't allowed" what? ("Allowed

her to bully you into changing your mind." *Season of Anomy,* p. 186.)

545.   "Scanning the surface of the tributary and around the confluence Ofeyi saw no evidence of" what? ("Of such desecration. The sandbanks gleamed spotlessly. Not even the usual patches of drying cassava roots could be seen—the settlements around were mostly alien and they were now deserted." *Season of Anomy,* p. 194.)

546.   "His expression did not change nor did he stop the entries he had been making in a large register when they arrived. Ofeyi was not even sure that he had" what? (He had looked up once since they entered the station." *Season of Anomy,* p. 202.)

547.   "On the route to the airport, about four miles out of town there is" what? ("There is a road which goes. Towards some agricultural settlements." *Season of Anomy,* p. 210.)

548.   "Ah yes of course. The great search for a woman. There was an awkward silence. The Dentist himself broke it by" what? ("By asking, 'Tell me, why is it important?" *Season of Anomy,* p. 218.)

549.   "I'll lie here some moment in time, labelled perhaps or without the sham of identity. Perhaps only with a filing number—date, place where picked up, by whom picked up…too late for" what? ("For it to matter then, at least not to me whom it really concerns." *Season of Anomy,* p. 226)

550.   "They were preparing to drive out of the station when Zaccheus pointed at a passing car and

said, 'That's the doc heading home. Man must be"
what? ("Man must be worked to death." *Season of
Anomy*, p. 234.)

551.　　"She shook her head. I don't believe that any
longer. It threatens to last a lifetime if" what? ("If life
is what I observe...what I have observed since I
came here. What I still see in you. Nothing that eats
the human life away has the smallest touch of
divinity." *Season of Anomy*, p. 242.)

552.　　"Good. Then perhaps whenever you are
forced to let off the first shot he can take that as a
signal to" what? ("To get I the car and dash off for
help." *Season of Anomy*, p. 250.)

553.　　"Hours later he walked from the loneliness of
his home to where the Ramaths lived. When. The
doctor asked him if his family had left he said yes,
they got" what? ("They got away safely." *Season of
Anomy*, p. 258.)

554.　　"Surprised but pleased, Taiila thanked him
but he continued, 'Not just beautiful but full of light.'
He glanced round the dank room. This room feels"
what? ("This room feels radiant, it must be your
presence." *Season of Anomy*, p. 266.)

555.　　"He rose. He reached outa. Hand to pat the
child on the head and" what? ("And stopped himself
in time. The gesture seemed grossly patronizing. He
walked on briskly to rejoin. The others." *Season of
Anomy*, p. 274.)

556.　　"The little man laughed. Red teeth. Black
gaps. You could tell" what? ("You could tell a

colanut addict. 'People outside think that this is a kind of morgue—abandon hope all who enter, something like that. But it isn't." *Season of Anomy,* p. 282.)

557.   "A new sound appeared to come from the ceiling fan, a mixture of asthmatic wheeze and a panting dog...Ofe turned round. It was only Suberu's unique way of breathing. Ofeyi stirred his cocoa aimlessly and" what? ("And sipped the tepid mixture." *Season of Anomy,* p. 290.)

558.   "It seems to be over, Karaun murmured rather dubiously. Again he clicked his fingers in the direction Suberu had gone as" what? ("As if by using his voice he would exacerbate the situation on the other side of the fence." *Season of Anomy,* p. 298.)

559.   "He did not move from the spot where he had regained consciousness, he lay still on the hard floor, his eyes turned" where? ("His eyes turned towards the camp-bed on to which Iriyise had been restored. No sign of the female nurse." *Season of Anomy,* p. 306.)

560.   "A stiffening from the giant alarmed Ofeyi and he sought frantically for a new idiom that would" what? ("A new idiom that would lessen the man's lifetime habit of suspicion." *Season of Anomy,* p. 315.)

Memoirs

XV. The Man Died: Prison Notes

561. "It is always a shock to encounter duplicate experiences in another being especially such experiences as reproduce near identical sensations, t thoughts, reactions and" what? ("And even expression in the other. For intimately felt experiences it is even a little frightening*." The Man Died: Prison Notes,* p. 11.)

562. "I experience this solidarity only with such of my people as share in this humiliation of tyranny. I exclude and ignore" what? ("And ignore all others. Whatever the factors that made a dictatorship inevitable in the first place, those factors no longer exist." *The Man Died: Prison Notes,* p. 15.)

563. "I have quoted Mangakis for the last time. The following is the text of the letter that still lies hidden" where? ("Hidden in the secret cabinets of today's national saviours." *The Man Died: Prison Notes,* p. 19.)

564. "The juxtaposition of these two sample events, even without" what? ("Without the reminder of its large-scale horror context, the most comprehensive, undiscriminating savaging of a people within memory on the black continent, destroys the hypocritical disclaimers of the regime." *The Man Died: Prison Notes,* pp. 23-24.)

565. "Next, the Ibadan Commissioner came in, apologetic. We were not going" where? ("To Dodan Barracks, the matter seemed to have been taken out

of his hands…he went on and on, barely coherent from emotional exhaustion." *The Man Died: Prison Notes,* p. 28.)

566.   "I have no idea whether or not a special squad was sent from Lagos. We asked for your arrest, maybe" what? ("Maybe that's what you heard about." *The Man Died: Prison Notes,* p. 32.)

567.   "I am seated in a spare office—on the floor above" what? ("Above the interrogation office." *The Man Died: Prison Notes,* p. 37.)

568.   "One night I had a weird, brief encounter. I had dozed off. Suddenly the door was flung open and" what? ("And a woman catapulted in." *The Man Died: Prison Notes,* p. 41.)

569.   "Apart from the NNDP embezzler there were" what? ("There were two more special class inmates. Detainees both." *The Man Died: Prison Notes,* p. 46.)

570.   "I know many loud-mouthed Nigerian patriots who would" what? ("Who would sell arms to Biafrans if they had a chance." *The Man Died: Prison Notes,* p. 50.)

571.   "The fight against the tyranny of the early sixties was greatly assisted by" whom? ("By policemen and officers who had uttered sentiments such as this." *The Man Died: Prison Notes,* p. 55.)

572.   "Then I understood his problem and laughed. 'Oh, I see, you think I have'" what? ("'I have been planted here to hear what you would say? I am not a

police informer.'" *The Man Died: Prison Notes,* p. 58.)

573.   "I rose as leisurely as I could and followed him at my own pace. It was next door, the library. Hardly had the door slammed shut than" what? ("Than it opened again and an officer was catapulted into the room to stay with ne." *The Man Died: Prison Notes,* p. 62.)

574.   "Predictably the police (and the government) panicked after" what? ("After the public episode at the hospital. They rushed to press the following day with a release which said, 'He sleeps well, eats well, is allowed to see his own doctor.'" *The Man Died: Prison Notes,* p. 67.)

575.   "One morning Security officers arrived at the prisons. I was taken into an office and" what? ("And, to my astonishment, fingerprinted." *The Man Died: Prison Notes,* p. 71.)

576.   "My first instinct was to ask. To see the Superintendent. I asked the warder to go for him and" what? ("And to emphasize the urgency, he left. I thought of what I would say to him to make him act at once on my proposed request for immediate transfer from that block." *The Man Died: Prison Notes,* p. 74.)

577.   "Confession—foiled escape—wail of humiliation. A trilogy aimed at the most cynical or blindly loyal mind. A beautiful logic all its own. A masterpiece of" what? ("Of credible fantasy calculated to shatter any lingering resistance to the

omnipotence of the regime." *The Man Died: Prison Notes,* p. 79.)

578.   "Response to my surroundings came slowly, the recognition of passing inmates as human beings, as" what? ("As individuals with unique features. That crisis was over." *The Man Died: Prison Notes,* p. 83.)

579.   "A private quest? Stuff for the tragic stage and the ritual rounds of Passion? A brave quest that" what? ("That diverges from, with never a backward glance at history's tramp of feet along the communal road? Is this then the long-threatened moment for jettisoning, for instance, notions of individual responsibility and the struggle it imposes? Must I now reject Kant? Karl Jaspers?" *The Man Died: Prison Notes,* p. 87.)

580.   "The effort at humour salvages yet another ghost, the time from the local pages of irony: Tony Enahoro, megaphone of" what? ("Megaphone of official falsehoods." *The Man Died: Prison Notes,* p. 91.)

581.   "You criminals, you have imbued your cause with unlimited power. Your contemptuous insight into the minds of" what? (Into the minds of a hysteria-manipulated mob has rendered too immune to further confrontation—this is your purpose and I acknowledge its present success." *The Man Died: Prison Notes,* pp. 94-95.)

582.   "Only to be returned to the same block in November. Upstairs and under lock and key. When that iron phase passed I went" where? ("I went into

the courtyard for exercise and spoke to them through the windows." *The Man Died: Prison Notes,* p. 98.)

583.   "The doors were locked on them. They pushed their food out of the cells untouched. In the afternoon the beans were" what? ("The beans were taken away and replaced by a soggy dough of farina and a lifeless incurable disease that went by the name of stew." *The Man Died: Prison Notes,* p. 103.)

584.   "The student continued: 'That was the picture that came to my mind. The picture of a quiet sadist who dined and'" what? ("'And wined and lulled himself to sleep with the sounds of the tortured.'" *The Man Died: Prison Notes,* p. 107.)

585.   "Almost simultaneously as the cell gates were opened the following morning came the question from everyone's lips, 'Did you hear them? Did you hear them last night?' And" what? ("And the accompanying response, 'I couldn't sleep. Even after they stopped I couldn't sleep." *The Man Died: Prison Notes,* p. 111.)

586.   "He protested, then, feeling that his life was in danger" did what? ("Deserted and fled to Lagos. He was arrested and incarcerated a week later." *The Man Died: Prison Notes,* p. 121.)

587.   "Water is the only exception to this body rejection. As rain from the sky or even at its most frozen in the marmattan I" what? ("I go under the showerless pipe and beat my brains into place beneath the force of a fireman's hose." *The Man Died: Prison Notes,* p. 131.)

588.   "The eyes suffer most from cold and dust. They have turned perpetually rheumy and the right one I fear is" what? ("Is impaired." *The Man Died: Prison Notes,* p. 141.)

589.   "Three weeks of books, then nothing! I had been so pleased with myself, the meeting with the Grand Zero had" what? ("Had yielded the all-important concessions on books." *The Man Died: Prison Notes,* p. 151.)

590.   "With its lapses, self-betrayals, incompletion, and ultimate desecration, was January 15th acceptable or not as" what? ("As a basis for a national struggle?" *The Man Died: Prison Notes,* p. 161.)

591.   "I was struck suddenly by the silence and the emptiness. Perhaps the empty feeling in me had" what? ("Had dulled my outer sensibility towards my surrounding." *The Man Died: Prison Notes,* p. 171.)

592.   "What God (white man) has put together, let no black man put asunder. The complications of neo-colonial politics of interference compel one to" what? ("To accept such a damnable catechism for now, as a pragmatic necessity." *The Man Died: Prison Notes,* p. 181.)

593.   "He turned blank. Never had I loathed the Asian accent as much has I did at that moment. As he spoke I recalled the entire history of" what? ("Of the Indo-Pakistani incursion into the Nigerian Civil Service, two departments mainly—the Railways and the Medical Services." *The Man Died: Prison Notes,* p. 191.)

594.   "A procession this morning on the others side of the floodhole. It has no precedent. I question it" how? ("Long and solemnly, ankle after ankle, chain by chain." *The Man Died: Prison Notes,* p. 201)

595.   "For a long time I looked down on the evidence, wondering how it came to be. For there it was, firmly rounded and taunt, an egg of" what? ("And egg of a protuberance that had no business on my waist-line" *The Man Died: Prison Notes,* p. 211.)

596.   "Tw omen were sent from Lagos, with the order. I heard there was some problem over how you were to get back to Lagos. I think they couldn't get" what? ("A plane or something." *The Man Died: Prison Notes,* p. 221.)

597.   "I waited for my news-clippings to arrive. Only that item really interested me know. I needed to check it against other reports. It could have been" what? ("A misquote." *The Man Died: Prison Notes,* p. 231.)

598.   "The first tool is the knife. It is the primal tool, the matrix of forms and shapes. That much is accepted, but I" what? ("I watched it happen, woke up one day to observe the evolution of the iron age and the liberation that dame from it in the cave man." *The Man Died: Prison Notes,* p. 241.)

599.   "It is strange, but the effect they all have on me is to" what? ("Is to resent even that cup of water. Each time the Grand Seer has turned up I have thrown the rest away." *The Man Died: Prison Notes,* p. 251.)

600.   "All souls congealment. All Souls meet in grey ghosts All Souls' Day and Night. All souls day after day, union, airless vault and cathedral gloom. Grease clouds of candles but not" what? (Not one flickering flame, not one tinted saint in leaded windows." *The Man Died: Prison Notes,* p. 261.)

XVI.   Ake': The Years of Childhood

601.   "The sprawling, undulating terrain is all of Ake. More than mere loyalty to the parsonage gave birth to "what? ("To a puzzle, and a resentment, that God should choose to look down on his own pious station, the parsonage compound, from the profane heights of Itoko." *Ake': The Years of Childhood,* p. 1.)

602.   "Well, you know your Uncle Sanya. He was angry. For one thing the best snails are" what? ("Are on the other side of that stream." *Ake': The Years of Childhood,* p. 6.)

603.   "And they would hear what sounded like" what? ("Like the slapping of wrists, a scrape of dishes on the ground or water slopping into a cup." *Ake': The Years of Childhood,* p. 11.)

604.   "I was not very sure. I could do that. Looking at her I wondered how Mrs B. coped with" what? ("With such a supernatural being who died, was re-born, died again and kept going and coming as often as she pleased." *Ake': The Years of Childhood,* p. 16.)

605.   "Not so fast. Let's go over God's injunction again…if thine right. Hand offendeth thee…note, offended thee…it says nothing about" what? ("About committing a sin." *Ake': The Years of Childhood,* p. 20.)

606.   "Finally, I stopped. I no longer saw Osiki but—Speed, Swiftness! I had not given any thought before then to "what? ("To the phenomenon of

human swiftness and Osiki's passage through the compound seemed little short of the magical." *Ake': The Years of Childhood,* p. 26.)

607.   "It seemed important to find out. The stained-glass windows behind the altar of St Peter's church displayed" what? ("Displayed the figures of three white men, dressed in robes which were very clearly egungun robes." *Ake': The Years of Childhood,* p. 32.)

608.   "I made a note to start learning how to ride a bicycle as we marched past" what? ("Marched past a bicycle hirer, busy mending a tube. A learner whose feet barely touched the pedals was just taking off, supported by a teacher who was no bigger but who appeared very full of instructions." *Ake': The Years of Childhood,* p. 38.)

609.   "One day, he fell off, right near us, at Ake. If we had been peeping over the wall at the time we would" what? ("We would have seen it happen. He was brought into our house where I heard someone explaining that his agbada has billowed out as usual until the sleeve was caught in the spokes of the wheel." *Ake': The Years of Childhood,* p. 44.)

610.   "Father laughed and said, 'Good idea. I'll get the stick. He whipped it out from its corner by his chair and handed it to" whom? ("To the bookseller's wife. The next moment, Mama was up and bounding through the parlour." *Ake': The Years of Childhood,* p. 50.)

611.   "Essay's laughter did not mean that there was definitely no reprimand to come. He remained in his

chair, very still. I felt him listening. Through the crack in the door I could" what? ("I could only see a thin line of his back, yet I knew he was listening for sounds of my movement in the pantry. We both knew the game." *Ake': The Years of Childhood,* p. 56.)

612.   "I never did discover how Adesina had lost his position with the Synod, and if he ever got it back. He left the house, like so many others before him, dejected, tearful. His eyes cast" what? ("His eyes cast a last appealing look at Wild Christian who had stayed on the periphery of the discussion; normally she would not even remain there, but the Synod somehow involved her as well since it was a church affair." *Ake': The Years of Childhood,* p. 62.)

613.   "The preceding moments regained focus. Yes, I had been sitting in the front room under the porcelain clock. I occupied the chair where visitors sat who had" what? ("Who had business with my father." *Ake': The Years of Childhood,* p. 68.)

614.   "It was close to midnight when Odejimi left the house that day, an exhausted, chastened teacher. Wild Christian did not" what? ("Did not broach the subject immediately; she merely served Essay his dinner, pretending not to understand the purpose of the quick survey which he made of the backyard when he returned, and the tight pursing of his lips on failing to see Le-moo anywhere." *Ake': The Years of Childhood,* p. 74.)

615.   "I had an ally. It was no more than a fleeting expression, and Essay never permitted himself more than that once to" what? ("To show disapproval. It was also likely that he did not really mind when the

exhibition took place among his 'own people'—like his debating circle—but once at last I caught him wince in discomfort then turn away to hide his distaste." *Ake': The Years of Childhood,* p. 80.)

616.   "Some processions however arrived for the church service already hymning or chanting refrains to prayers or other mutterings by a robed cleric who led" what? ("Who led the procession or brought up the rear." *Ake': The Years of Childhood,* p. 86.)

617.   "When I sneaked out later, not much later, the bundle was gone. Joseph had found it, had picked it up and" what? ("And restored its contents where they belonged." *Ake': The Years of Childhood,* p. 92.)

618.   "The flimsier structures of Ake, built of unbaked mud could not stand up to the rains of July and August. The corrugated iron sheets were penetrated by the wind which ripped them off, flung them over other roofs, leaving the rain to "what? ("To find the weakest point in the walls, dissolve the mud and flush out the household." *Ake': The Years of Childhood,* p. 98.)

619.   "Dipo's howls had gone down, and Joseph came out. It could have been my imagination, but I felt that he deliberately gave me a wide berth. His words however left him in" what? (In no doubt about how he felt. To ensure that he was at most cutting, he did not even design to address me directly; indeed I now understood why he had cut such a wide curve around me." *Ake': The Years of Childhood,* p. 104.)

620.   "When dey come Mama, dem go know say there be black man medicine. I go pile dem corpse

alongside the wall of dis place, dem go know say we" what? ("Say we done dey fight war here, long time before dey know wetin be war for den foolish land." *Ake': The Years of Childhood,* p. 110.)

621.	"He was short, rather light-complexioned and had a small, box-like head. HM's regimen was to go to the school to conduct the opening, then" what? ("Then return home for a leisurely breakfast. By the, Wild Christian would be in her shop." *Ake': The Years of Childhood,* p. 116.)

622.	"The stranger did not give chase. Instead he remained on the spot and seemed to sway a little. His eyes appeared to be fused with his spectacles so that what struck me most was" what? ("Was that his face glowed centrally through a pair of head lamps, like a motor-car." *Ake': The Years of Childhood,* p. 122.)

623.	"My father shook his head, gestured with open hands that he had nothing to do with it. Odemo's voice had" what? ("Had made me turn to look at him, then rough the room at a surprising identity of expressions of the faces of all the guests. Suddenly confused, I fled from the room and ran all the way back home." *Ake': The Years of Childhood,* p. 128.)

624.	"I launched my pebble at the same time as Temi threw his, saw mine rise barely up. To the level of the lowest branch before" what? ("Before commending its journey back to earth." *Ake': The Years of Childhood,* p. 134.)

625.	"No. What some of them don't know is that if we fight, we get punished. Any time we return home with torn clothes or somebody reports" what? ("Or somebody reports that we have been in a fight we get punished." *Ake': The Years of Childhood,* p. 140.)

626. "A soothing band encased my ankle. When I looked down I noticed" what? ("I noticed a wide swathe in the mixture of the dish. Binding my ankle now was the strip of cloth which had been soaked in that mixture." *Ake': The Years of Childhood,* p. 146.)

627. "But the seasonal anthems rehearsed by the choir also exerted my voice. The tunes came out clearly enough, but not" what? ("But not the words. These emerged as some strange language, a mixture of English, Yoruba and some celestial language that could only be what was spoken by those cherubs in the stained-glass windows, whose mouths sprouted leaves and branches as they circled the beatific faces of saints and archangels." *Ake': The Years of Childhood,* p. 152.)

628. "The even created some consternation among the mango-tree population. Our own pupils at St Peter brought" what? ("Brought back daily news of the progress of this liaison between the two outcasts, and the reactions of the food-sellers and their customers." *Ake': The Years of Childhood,* p. 158.)

629. "Grandfather was right, they were not all men at Ageokuta Grammar School—AGS to most of Abekuta—but there were" what? ("There were numbers whose only distinguishing feature from teachers was that they wore the blue shirts and khaki-khaki uniforms of the schoolboys. In every other aspect they were ready to be heads of their own

households, and some of them already were." *Ake':
The Years of Childhood,* p. 164.)

630.   "In AGS however, grass took on 'good' and
'bad' definitions. It was not just a question of weeds
or dangerous kinds of grass with" what? ("With.
thorns or with sharp or stubby roots." *Ake': The
Years of Childhood,* p. 170.)

631.   "One chicken between three fully grown
boys for seven days? It sounded inadequate. I
wondered if they wouldn't have preferred to" what?
("Preferred to be beaten and given other tasks to
perform." *Ake': The Years of Childhood,* p. 176.)

632.   "The voice was none other than Kemberi's.
The junior 'wives' of a household and a mischievous
lot I reflected, to so name a woman whose real name,
and a Christian one at that, waws Amelia. To the
women's gathering this highly feared, fearless and
voluble woman might be" whom? ("Might be
Madame Amelia, but about the time that I became a
limpet on the group." *Ake': The Years of Childhood,*
p. 182.)

633.   "It was a grim reception awaiting the boy in
whose luggage these items had been found. While I
was a willing participant in the search. I was rather
dubious about" what? ("About the rightness of
actually confronting the pair with our trophy." *Ake':
The Years of Childhood,* p. 188.)

634.   "There was no time to lose. Daodu now took
over the direction of arrangements for" what? ("For
welcoming back his Beere from England. He

overlooked no detail." *Ake': The Years of Childhood,* p. 194.)

635.   "Some young, radical nationalists were being gaoled for sedition, and sedition had become equivalent to" what? ("To demanding that the white man leave us to rule ourselves. New names came fore and more to the fore." *Ake': The Years of Childhood,* p. 200.)

636.   "It was this scene that came most clearly to mind as I" what? ("As I turned aside half a mile before the CMS bookshop to take a short cut which took me to the rear of St Peter's parsonage, through the cemetery, then through the school compound, through Bishops Court, emerging by the rear gate opposite Pa Solotan's house, then round the back of the church to Wild Christian's shop, stopping to pass the news to Bunmi who was on duty at the time." *Ake': The Years of Childhood,* p. 206.)

637.   "What happened next, was impossible to predict. I had retreated to the edge of the field but" what? ("But remained close to the office blocks, fearful now of being trampled to death." *Ake': The Years of Childhood,* p. 212)

638.   "The women now dug in for a long siege. Shock squads roamed the city, mobilizing all womanhood. Markets and women's shops were" what? ("Were ordered closed. Those who defied the order had their goods confiscated and sent to the field before the palace." *Ake': The Years of Childhood,* p. 218.)

639.   "Her face became more and more agitated as she listened, then broke in again. Yes, you know damned well what you should have done if you" what? ("If you sincerely desired their surrender. You could have dropped it on one of their mountains, even in the sea, anywhere where they could see what would happened if they persisted in the war, but you chose instead to drop in on peopled cities." *Ake': The Years of Childhood,* p. 224.)

640.   "I was no longer paying attention. My eyes had swiveled slowly to encounter Beere's who was" what? ("Who was grinning with her eyebrows raised in mock distress. The sight was so comical that I burst out laughing and she joined in, leaving Daodu glancing from one to the other, frowning in his attempt to recollect what he had said that was so funny. Tiling her voice in sympathy Beer queried." *Ake': The Years of Childhood,* p. 230.)

XVII. Isara: A Voyage Around Essay

641. "Ashtabula!! Soditan eased out the envelope with foreign stamps, addressed in a bold, sweeping cursive. It was already slit open, and as he released the neatly folded sheets, his spare frame responded to" what? ("To the emerging treat and he visibly related." *Isara: A Voyage around Essay,* p. 3.)

642. "Ashtabula was a private world, one which he kept secure even from the close circle of the ex-Iles. From time to time he would" what? ("He would 'lend' them a portion of that world, a portion too immense to keep within Isara." *Isara: A Voyage around Essay,* p. 9.)

643. "The monster steadily belched out its own entrails and was in turn" what? ("Was in turn swallowed by them." *Isara: A Voyage around Essay,* p. 14.)

644. "Pushing his way through with his long arms, on short bandy legs, Damian was" what? ("Was already at the entrance to the station building, but he did not remain within it, since Yode saw him shortly reappear behind the building, duck beneath an open window, thinking he was unobserved, then vanish altogether between what looked like a row of kiosks and prefabricated dwellings." *Isara: A Voyage around Essay,* p. 20.)

645. "Damian's eyes opened wide. 'Ask you to come? You! Do you know where you are going? Let me tell you, you think they have pito there? Ho, let me tell you, my brother is" where? ("My brother is in one of those places, there is one in Ughelli, not

much different from the one you'll be attending, judging from what I hear." *Isara: A Voyage around Essay,* p. 24.)

646.   "Wemiuja intervened with definitive authority. "Ford is all right for passenger lorry, Baba, or Bedford, But for timber, you need" what? ("You need engine like Commer."' *Isara: A Voyage around Essay,* p. 28.)

647.   "Akinyode stared hard at the smoke-rimed rafters, thinking of this new. imposition on his resources. No one had "what? ("No one had discussed it with him." *Isara: A Voyage around Essay,* p. 32.)

648.   "All in all, yes, he found himself in agreement with" what? ("With the white-haired patron-the school as the 'factory of humanity,' in which 'teachers are'" what? ("'Teachers are the artisangs.'" *Isara: A Voyage around Essay,* p. 36.)

649.   "Of all the debates ever embarked upon by the ex-Iles, this had" what? ("This had proved one of the most intense, certainly the most prolonged." *Isara: A Voyage around Essay,* p. 40.)

650.   "Admit it now, Soditan murmured to himself as his eyelids finally began to" what? ("To droop and he. Turned the lampwick down for the last time that night, it was not…no, he intended to be scrupulously fair to himself…it was only partly the travelogues of Cudeback and his chance encounter with the Mussolini-Hauptmann dialogue which spurred his bicycle excursion to Iseyin." *Isara: A Voyage around Essay,* p. 44,)

651.   "He had shown the greatest promise, and Dr Mackintosh has remarked him to "whom? ("To his colleagues." *Isara: A Voyage around Essay,* p. 48.)

652.   "But these were small, dilettante beginnings; now it was time to move on and" what? ("And win more territory, challenge the Lebanese and Indiana traders who monopolized the cloth trade." *Isara: A Voyage around Essay,* p. 52)

653.   "Sipe's self-recrimination knew no bounds, taking on himself the blame for" what? ("For his predicament—even including the breakdown of the vehicle." *Isara: A Voyage around Essay,* p. 56.)

654.   "Among that circle of friends, however, Otuyemi was a poor performer, and Sipe thought nothing of" what? ("Of helping him with his homework. From homework to class tests to examination was a progression that developed without much. Thought." *Isara: A Voyage around Essay,* p. 60.)

655.   "Efuape re-read the contents of the paper. Onayemi had prepared the conjuring brief, based on" what? ("On his prior experiences in this kind of affair." *Isara: A Voyage around Essay,* p. 64.)

656.   "Right, he said, now we know who the Antichrist is—you saw him turn tail, didn't you? By their tails—and" what? ("And cloven hooves—we shall know them." *Isara: A Voyage around Essay,* p. 68.)

657. "Mariam shifted the bolt of mat in the corner of the room listlessly, without even "what? ("Without even looking down into the vacated space. To her husband, Josiah, the lone witness of her futile search. It was clear that she had no further interest in the result. Of her motions or, at least, no further expectations, and Josiah lost his temper." *Isara: A Voyage around Essay,* p. 73.)

658. "She got up then, set down the porridge pot and" what? ("And flicked the ladle to get rids of the drips. She cleaned the ladle further with her forefinger, and her tongue pronounced it pleasantly burnt." *Isara: A Voyage around Essay,* p. 77.)

659. "She felt better. A sense of loneliness reduced meant even that her problems were nearly solved. She placed the modest fee on the table. It was time to" what? ("To turn her mind to other matters that Tenten's death had provoked." *Isara: A Voyage around Essay,* p. 81.)

660. "It was the longest silence ever, and Mariam found herself the entre of unaccustomed turmoil in the Bible class. Catechist Aderounmu, transferred to Isara barely three months before, began to wonder if" what? ("If he had been thrown, unprotected, into the very tower of Babel." *Isara: A Voyage around Essay,* p. 85.)

661. "Josiah shook his head. 'I am a Christian. I even hold a title in the church. Just think how it would sound when it is found out that I'" what? ("'That I took my in-law to Ogboni for burial.'" *Isara: A Voyage around Essay,* p. 89.)

662.   "This time the other man spoke. 'We cannot bury Tenten but his is our death. We have sent for those who will'" what? ("'Who will bury him. Send the egunsale to us at Iledi and all the rites will be performed. Later, someone will take you to where he has been buried.'" *Isara: A Voyage around Essay,* p. 92)

663.   "Graciously, the teacher conceded that the Genie's presence was quite superfluous; his will to continue his work was already fully subverted. To his caller, however, he said" what? ("Not looking up from his desk, 'You are not here. I merely sighed and you appeared. All I have to do is sigh again and you will vanish." *Isara: A Voyage around Essay,* p. 96.)

664.   "He had one handicap, however, and it was one which the boy could not overcome. His father was" what? ("His father was a first cousin to the head teacher." *Isara: A Voyage around Essay,* p. 100.)

665.   "That's what he says. And he says that's why I shall die a teacher, and as poor as a church mouse. He says in one breath, then tries to" what? ("To save me from myself in the next mail." *Isara: A Voyage around Essay,* p. 104.)

666.   "After that, they both fell silent. He kept" what? ("He kept the pen poised over the writing pad, his mind busy on the best phrasing to mollify his father; the letter had to be ready for the courier who would leave very early in the morning." *Isara: A Voyage around Essay,* p. 113.)

667.   "He took up his pen and prepared a draft response to his query. It stated" what? ("The facts

very simply and reiterated his view that Akanbi's conduct merited instant dismissal from the school; he had been flogged as a lesser punishment." *Isara: A Voyage around Essay,* p. 121.)

668.   "All right. What do you want us to do? Of course, he casually added, as you yourself have just advised, Morola won't" what? ("Morola won't be traveling anywhere for some time." *Isara: A Voyage around Essay,* p. 130.)

669.   "Yes, just imagine my feelings! I would have stayed behind to welcome you. Oh, I felt" how? ("I felt so cheated!" *Isara: A Voyage around Essay,* p. 138.)

670.   "Yes, it's sad." Why? ("When someone in such a position throws away his future just like that!" *Isara: A Voyage around Essay,* p. 147.)

671.   "The door was flung open and a compact tornado erupted into the room. Neither of the two young men expected" whom? ("Pa Josiah. Seasonal homecoming, as this was, generally meant that he would abandon his home completely to his son and his friends, taking refuge with his wives in turn, but mostly staying with Jagun." *Isara: A Voyage around Essay,* p. 155.)

672.   "The second development was truly dramatic. Akinkore finally presented" what? ("A sample of typical missionary dialogue—as he explained to the meeting." *Isara: A Voyage around Essay,* p. 163.)

673.   "Opeilu's fever was prolonged, even though he had to report to work every day. He wore" what? ("He wore a thick scarf around his neck, and a generous whiff of mentholatum surrounded his presence." *Isara: A Voyage around Essay,* p. 172.)

674.   "Everything combines. Together for good for the righteous man. Sipe pontificated, steering" what? ("Steering Morris over Carter Bridge into Lagos Island." *Isara: A Voyage around Essay,* p. 180.)

675.   "The carpenter went into a torrent of excuses, barely understandable, but related to Tenten's death and" what? ("And a message from his sister Mariam." *Isara: A Voyage around Essay,* p. 189.)

676.   "The master driver's face relaxed into" what? ("Into a satisfied grin, swiftly followed by" what? ("By a spasm of anguish as he remembered what had caused his presenct there." *Isara: A Voyage around Essay,* p. 197.)

677.   "Then we can't waste any more time. The Agunrin is" what? ("Is the one we must tackle. He has the longest memory, and that is what fuels the violence. Memory can be a dangerous thing in a stubborn old man." *Isara: A Voyage around Essay,* p. 205.)

678.   "Until his figure was swallowed up in the dark the boy stood" where? ("At the door, staring at his hero turned philanthropist." *Isara: A Voyage around Essay,* p. 215.)

679.   "And then Josiah cursed himself for a fool and told the women" what? ("To go home. There was

nothing to worry about." *Isara: A Voyage around Essay,* p. 225.)

680.　　　"And it soon became clear that the homage was cast" how? ("Wider, that it embraced more than the rider." *Isara: A Voyage around Essay,* p. 235.)

XVIII. Ibadan: The Penkelemes Years:
A memoir, 1946-1967

681.   "Homecoming was, at the time, so ordinary, so uneventful that even he felt dissatisfied. Something was" what? ("Something was missing. This end to a five-year absence, a fifth, nearly, of his entire life, lacked some form of rounding-off, a ritual resonance that would echo, even as it reversed, the excited, yet unformed longings that surrounded his departure." *Ibadan: The Penkelemes Years,* p. 1.)

682.   "Autumn in Europe was the closest to his season, but the Harmattan lacked" what? ("Lacked its chromatic rave that slowly, with such tenacious protest, weakened in stages and fell to earth, curling inwards. To brown deaths to be swept into brief mounds by wind or broom." *Ibadan: The Penkelemes Years,* p. 11.)

683.   "The name your godmother stuck you with. I think you've been" what? ("Been too long away and have forgotten the right intonation, a which means of course, you've lost the correct meant." *Ibadan: The Penkelemes Years,* p. 20.)

684.   "For the stranger from colonial Nigeria, this was no longer an anonymous voice from Little Mo, Mississippi, any more than" who ("Any more than Billie Holiday or Leadbelly." *Ibadan: The Penkelemes Years,* p. 30.)

685.   "Rapidly, he performed some mental calculations, then headed for the Left Bank, thanking his stars that he had" what? ("That he had previously undertaken the hitch-hike to Paris after the hard but

quite enjoyable labour in Lyon." *Ibadan: The Penkelemes Years,* p. 39.)

686.   "Never, Maren would later admit, had his reflexes worked with such perfect coordination. Only Tomas was left standing, still going krr-ke-ke-ke, seemingly" what? ("Seemingly oblivious to the rapidity with which the gendarme had readied his gun and was now pointing it directly at him." *Ibadan: The Penkelemes Years,* p. 47.)

687.   "The visitor rose, gratefully, even with relief. He was not, after all, about to be" what? ("To be flayed in the secrecy of a Claridges suite, packaged in a diplomatic bag and dumped in the Seine." *Ibadan: The Penkelemes Years,* p. 56.)

688.   "His installation was separate from the Independence celebrations. These had not only been opulent and magnificent, they had" what? ("They had narrowly escaped sabotage in the form of a play entitled *A Dance of the Forests* which had been thoughtlessly selected by a jury as befitting a nation's rite of passage." *Ibadan: The Penkelemes Years,* p. 65.)

689.   "None of these affectations diminished the anticipation of" what? ("Of the gathered company as she walked onto the stage for her first number, an aria from *Madame Butterfly" Ibadan: The Penkelemes Years,* p. 73.)

690.   "A pained look in his face, the father spoke tersely. 'I really don't see' what? ("'I don't see how the two things are connected. Your mother wants tp know how the minister reacted and all you do is keep

harping on who brought us into the worrying business."' *Ibadan: The Penkelemes Years,* p. 82.)

691.   "His levitating session ended abruptly and he winced at the unpleasant thought: suppose they: what? ("Suppose they choose to come in person?" *Ibadan: The Penkelemes Years,* p. 90.)

692.   "The senior boy misread the puzzlement on the newcomer's face, and leant forward, hopefully. 'Or perhaps you do not quite understand: Your physiognomy has'" what? ("'Has taken on the appearance of bewilderment.'" *Ibadan: The Penkelemes Years,* p. 99.)

693.   "Perhaps the relief and the euphoria of the following morning had something to do with it. Komi lived in Greer House but, to simplify catering and" what? ("And discipline during half-term, everyone had been moved to Swanston." *Ibadan: The Penkelemes Years,* p. 107.)

694.   "It did not take long for the race for a pecking order to commence. An offense strangely taken, a flurry of blows, a harmless exchange turned into "what? ("Into a declaration of war…any excuse to magnify a slight, real or contrived, and he soon found himself a bewildered participant in sudden, impromptu bouts." *Ibadan: The Penkelemes Years,* p. 116.)

695.   "It was not the apple that tempted Eve, but" what? ("But the grapefruit; thus did Maren revise the tale of paradise lost, and even Christ, shocked as he was at such blasphemy, confessed himself tempted to agree whenever Maren returned from raiding the

Principal's compound, with a shirtful of the booty to share, especially on a hot afternoon." *Ibadan: The Penkelemes Years,* p. 125.)

696.   "Confident in the sanctuary of the library, Maren laughed. 'Teach me a lesson, you? It is I should teach you. You need" what? ("You need teaching 'Deyelu, your mind needs improving.'" *Ibadan: The Penkelemes Years,* p. 133.)

697.   "Still, it had to be an ill wind that blew no one any good, and those more knowledgeable in the ways of the bush, and" what? ("And lacking any inhibition, waited a while for the earth to cool down, then began to forage." *Ibadan: The Penkelemes Years,* p. 141.)

698.   "His attention was first caught by the attractive cover of" what? ("Of a slim book, rather the worse for wear thanks to the activities of cockroaches." *Ibadan: The Penkelemes Years,* p. 150.)

699.   "You…like to provoke me, 'Kinkoyi. If you have something against me, say it now. Don't think I haven't" what? ("Don't think I haven't noticed. You have something against me, so have the courage to say it. to my face." *Ibadan: The Penkelemes Years,* p. 158.)

700.   "Once upon a time there was only Yaba Higher College, in Lagos. It was a place of" what? ("Of learned mystery from where emerged serious-looking men and a handful of women, who would later populate the teaching profession in choice secondary schools; occupy the few senior positions in the civil service that were permitted to non-

Europeans, better known as natives; become pharmacists in government hospitals, land surveyors or public engineers,; or acquire the preliminary medical training that might later take them to Glasgow, Dublin or London to be transformed into fully-fledged doctors." *Ibadan: The Penkelemes Years,* p. 167.)

701.　"This knife had remarkable balance, a feature which the main enthusiast had" what? ("Had long discovered, making him very proficient in the new sport." *Ibadan: The Penkelemes Years,* p. 175)

702.　"A willowy being like Adelugba, but taller, his gentle face belief the toughness that appeared to be" what? ("That appeared to be the standard armoury of the juju and high-life nightclub bandmen." *Ibadan: The Penkelemes Years,* p. 183.)

703.　"Maren was grateful that the Ihiala festival was over, and he dragged his truck" where? (Back to Ibadan, arriving after dark." *Ibadan: The Penkelemes Years,* p. 192.)

704.　"Not so universally relished was a depiction of the climbdown and evident importance of" whom" ("Of the father of the nation, Nnamdi Azikiwe, in a subsequent tussle with his Prime Minister, Tafawa Balewa." *Ibadan: The Penkelemes Years,* p. 200.)

705.　"A lull in activities, a motor vehicle would come roaring in and they would take off again not always all at once, and sometimes only for" what? (Only for short spells." *Ibadan: The Penkelemes Years,* p. 209.)

706.   "It was a pained silence that followed. Yes, Maren felt he understood only too well what was being said, which was" what? ("Which was that was being left unsaid." *Ibadan: The Penkelemes Years*, p. 219.)

707.   "No matter, he drove his wife, not even to a hospital but all the way to "where? ("To the seat of Government, Ibadan, where he was an honourable member of the House of Assembly, led her violated body into the headquarters of law enforcement and made her tell her story." *Ibadan: The Penkelemes Years*, p. 229.)

708.   "Chief S. L. Akintola was tickled. 'So he is now a bloodthirsty animal? When he banned his bloodthirsty dramatic sketches against us, and we decided to take action, weren't you the same person who began preaching'" what? ("'At us the sermon of free speech?'" *Ibadan: The Penkelemes Years*, p. 238.)

709.   "Nor did he experience any particular surprise that Kodak stood up as soon as" what? ("As soon as he reached his table, his mouth agape, half the side of a grasscutter sticking out of his mouth." *Ibadan: The Penkelemes Years*, p. 249.)

710.   "Oh yes, I'd forgotten all about that. He waved his hand in the general direction of" what ("In the general direction of a stack of books and records. 'Maybe you'll find something in there to suit your needs." *Ibadan: The Penkelemes Years*, p. 259.)

711.   "In Habana once, a middle-aged man looked at him with disapproval, the cause of offence being"

what? ("Being the miserable tuft on his chin. Why he demanded, was he wearing a beard?" *Ibadan: The Penkelemes Years,* p. 269.)

712. "Impressarios, Maren held, must be beings of infinite patience, but perhaps they" what? ("Perhaps they merely feigned such patience until they got what they wanted and they, heaven help even the genius who had led them a merry dance, played hard to get, or merely acted the prima donna." *Ibadan: The Penkelemes Years,* p. 279.)

713. "Finally, Maren kept watch and, sure enough, the sleek coil emerged in the morning somewhere from, it seemed, the floorboards" and what? ("Slithered its way through the sparse foliage that grew around the house, vanished into the bush. In the evening, it returned the same way." *Ibadan: The Penkelemes Years,* p. 289.)

714. "The officer sighed and shook his head. 'You University people, you are so remote from what goes on The Deputy Commissioner did not bother to ask for our statement because'" why? ("'Because he does not really need it." *Ibadan: The Penkelemes Years,* p. 299.)

715. "His interlocutor had not hit him; perhaps he was the head guard and such menial duties were" what? ("Were left to his subordinates. Mo matter, this figure, with his stick loosely held, was the only clear object Maren could see beneath the flailing sticks." *Ibadan: The Penkelemes Years,* p. 309.)

716. "I'm not so sure, Komo persisted. The feudal alliance has definitely marked down Lagos for its

own; Biobaku may prove to be" what? ("To be only a holding device. They probably have their real candidate waiting on the sidelines." *Ibadan: The Penkelemes Years,* p. 319.)

717.   "He recognized it was a lie. The tall masts and criss-crossing wires around the building were not there for nothing. He moved close to the face he had easily identified as sympathetic, someone who" what? ("Someone who acted as if he was carrying out a distasteful duty." *Ibadan: The Penkelemes Years,* p. 329.)

718.   "Maren had agreed with his associates that this bastion of state propaganda was" what? ("Was both a legitimate and a feasible target." *Ibadan: The Penkelemes Years,* p. 339.)

719.   "Once in the toilet, Maren felt an overwhelming sense of the ridiculous at what he knew he was about to do. There was, however, no time to waste. On no account could" what? ("On no account could the transmitter be permitted to leave Ibadan; indeed, to leave that house, since looking for a new location, then setting it up, and renewing contracts, would consume valuable time." *Ibadan: The Penkelemes Years,* p. 349.)

720.   "I was not alone there, you know. Quite a few of us felt that way, and not just from Nigeria. It was South Africa, South Africa all the way: you can't imagine" what? ("You can't imagine the idealism." *Ibadan: The Penkelemes Years,* p. 380.)

XIX. You Must Set Forth at Dawn

721.   "Outside myself at moments like this, heading home, I hesitate a moment to check" what? ("To check if it is a truly living me. Perhaps I am just. A disembodied self usurping my body, strapped into a business class seat in the plane, being borne to my designated burial ground—the cactus patch on the grounds of my home in Abeokuta, a mere hour's escape by road from the raucous heart of Lagos." *You Must Set Forth At Dawn,* p.)

722.   "Reasonable? Were we being unreasonable? After nearly thirty years of military rule, the last five under the most repellent of the species, we were asking for" what? ("For the immediate release of the elected president and all remaining political prisoners and the setting up of an interim government headed by Abiola, the legitimate president—an interim government that would las a year, maybe two." *You Must Set Forth At Dawn,* p. 17.)

723.   "For nearly the last five years of his life, Fela was fully convinced not only that he was a reincarnated Egyptian god but that he had" what? ("But that he had actually begun to reverse the aging process and would again revert to childhood and infancy." *You Must Set Forth At Dawn,* p. 29.)

724.   "Given the unpredictable situation in Hungary, the uncertainty of my position resulted in my writing a rare letter to Essay—my father—taking him into my confidence. It seemed only fair, in case" what? ("In case I was wounded, taken prisoner, or worse." *You Must Set Forth At Dawn,* p. 41.)

725.   "When I returned to Nigeria on New Year's Day 1960, it was a nation wound up to a fever pitch of" what? ("Of social expectations—and self-confidence—as its date for independence from British rule drew close. Its future was already mapped out, however, for the eve-of-independence elections had taken place the previous year, and all that was left for the British government to hand over power to the victorious party and take its leave." *You Must Set Forth At Dawn,* p. 53.)

726.   "The 'roaring sixties' were not, however, an unbroken period of political outrage and response, of impositions, of a" what? ("Of a bleak intensity that sometimes appeared to have dominated, even defined, the life of a young man of thirty." *You Must Set Forth At Dawn,* p. 65.)

727.   "'Bourgeois' was also enemy territory in the United States of the 1960s and was sometimes interchangeable with" what? ("With 'white,' 'racist,' segregationist'—against all of which the black writers were producing a powerful body of revolutionary work." *You Must Set Forth At Dawn,* p. 77.)

728.   "The formal security around me grew quite slack as the case wore on. For instance, a famous picture—it appeared also in foreign newspapers—showed me being" what? ("Being escorted across the road from my police cell by one policeman only, unarmed." *You Must Set Forth At Dawn,* p. 89.)

729.   "And there, with the shift of power, the nation hoped" what? ("The nation hoped that the

bloodletting would cease—but no." *You Must Set Forth At Dawn,* p. 101.)

730.   "The center was funded mainly by an American foundation, the Farfield, that was later proven to be" what? ("To be affiliated with the CIA, though none of us knew it then." *You Must Set Forth At Dawn,* p. 113.)

731.   "In his position as commissioner for information, Tony Enahoro was the government spokesman who would" what? ("Who would read to the international press, after my arrest and detention, an infamous confessional statement that had me admitting that I had been negotiating the purchase of warplanes for Biafra!? *You Must Set Forth At Dawn,* p. 125.)

732.   "The moment came when everyone, even the most ardent optimist, knew that Victor Banjo would" what? ("Would never make that crossing to Lagos." *You Must Set Forth At Dawn,* p. 137.)

733.   "Such dehumanization of the populace did not take place only at checkpoints that were formally manned, but these were" what? ("These were the most public places, and their audiences were guaranteed to cover the entire gamut of civil life." *You Must Set Forth At Dawn,* p. 149.)

734.   "Looking back, it strikes me with some astonishment that, until his death in 1987, one constant, a large presence in the 'extracurricular' undertakings of my adult existence, was" who? ("Olufemi Babington Johnson. Just who was this being?" *You Must Set Forth At Dawn,* p. 163.)

735.   "The university itself was a water-lapped oasis despite the choice of" what? ("Despite the choice of a ponderous boathouse architecture for its main buildings." *You Must Set Forth At Dawn,* p. 173.)

736.   "The saga has not ended. Fate again intervenes, and the hero finds himself" how? ("Arraigned before a brutal dictator, one General Sani Abacha, on treasonable charges, earning a death sentence that will be commuted to a lengthy prison spell." *You Must Set Forth At Dawn,* p. 185.)

737.   "Back on campus, I plunged int the surrounding bush for" what? ("For the routine of sorting out my thoughts. It was clear that for the recovery of Ori Olokun, I was prepared to dine with the lord of the satanic kingdom himself, even without the aid of the long spoon. I was more than ready to make a Faustian pact—to sell my soul in return for that hollow but weighty mass, hallowed by my history!" *You Must Set Forth At Dawn,* p. 197.)

738.   "Our planes did not cross paths over the Atlantic—not quite. Later, as we conducted a detailed postmortem on the sequence of events, followed up on the actions of the police and the departure of Pierre, we discovered" what? ("We discovered that we had actually been in Rio de Janeiro—in the departure section of the airport—at the very moment that Pierre was passing through to Immigration and baggage claim. Fifteen minutes either way, and the two gladiatorial groups would have encountered each other, perhaps in the parking lot or at the frontage of the airport building!" *You Must Set Forth At Dawn,* p. 209.)

739.   "Pierre died some years ago. Reconciliation with that misused scholar was one that I truly craved, but" what? ("But appeasement must now be delayed until our reunion under the generous canopy of Orunmila." *You Must Set Forth At Dawn,* p. 221.)

740.   "What shocked me, however, as we returned our captive to his venue, was that, despite nearly two hours' absence, all the guests had" what? ("All the guests had remained in their position. I had not anticipated this. If the guest of honor vanishes and all eating and speechifying is over, the obvious course of action is—go home!" *You Must Set Forth At Dawn,* p. 233.)

741.   "His enthusiasm was infectious. We would pool our resources. I would not only make the call but would" what? ("I would co-opt Ojetunji Aboyade to follow up the case after our visit." *You Must Set Forth At Dawn,* p. 245.)

742.   "The aparo survived. If the coup makers had only taken the trouble to consult me, I would have advised" what? ("I would have advised them that his fate was already decried in those scattered feathers, which were all that remained when the Artful Dodger fell to a dramatist's gun but remained destined for the greatest escapist performance of his career." *You Must Set Forth At Dawn,* p. 257.)

743.   "Liston was, of course, a different setting and a far more composed affair: a North-South dialogue. It seemed a perfect pointer. If North and Sough could dialogue, so could" whom? ("So could South and South or, in my mediate context, ANC and Inkatha." *You Must Set Forth At Dawn,* p. 269.)

151

744.   "Years later, President Francois Mitterrand conferred on me the prestigious title of Chevalier de la Legion d'Honneur. The ceremony was conducted by "whom? ("By his ambassador in Nigeria." *You Must Set Forth At Dawn,* p. 281.)

745.   "Of course it feels grand and comparatively stress-free to work occasionally in theaters where everything is predictable—the stage mechanics work, actors are paid, there is" what? ("There is a set division of labor and so on—but I confess that such ventures leave me hankering for the more precarious existence that is not so much a noun as it is a verb; theater is where theater happens." *You Must Set Forth At Dawn,* p. 292.)

746.   "George Bernard Shaw is reputed to have said, 'I find it easy to forgive the man who invented a devilish instrument like dynamite, but how can one ever forgive the diabolical mind that'" what? ("'That invented the Nobel Prize in Literature.'" *You Must Set Forth At Dawn,* p. 305.)

747.   "Some, it was true, and in quite respectable quarters, considered his relationship with the government" how? ("Rather ambiguous—for no discernible reason." *You Must Set Forth At Dawn,* p. 317.)

748.   "I cut short my merriment. 'I am laughing at you because you'" what? ("'You dare take me for a moron. You actually expect me to leave the safety of. my room to come and confront you, a total stranger in a strange hotel in the middle of the night? Now, listen, I am going to put down the phone, and if you dare all back again, I guarantee you'll sleep in a

police cell tonight.'" *You Must Set Forth At Dawn*, p. 329.)

749.   "Now I stood alone on a mound of gravel, surveying my domain wistfully, wondering how soon I might see it finally materialize into "what? ("Into the edifice I could pictures so clearly in my mind." *You Must Set Forth At Dawn*, p. 341.)

750.   "He led the way to where a solitary driver had remained in his taxi, doors wide open and" what? ("And the seat flattened out as far as it would go, fast asleep." *You Must Set Forth At Dawn*, p. 353.)

751.   "I appeared to have entered a war zone, the scene of recent battles, mostly one-side. Corpses littered the streets, casualties with" what? ("With horrifying wounds, and patches of caked blood discolored the tar and sometimes the gray concrete divider on the motorway." *You Must Set Forth At Dawn*, p. 365.)

752.   "In August 1994, surrounded and menaced by fully armed and kitted mobile police who pressed their aces against windows and" what? ("And a metal grilled that surrounded the open assembly hall, I held a press conference at the Mayflower School, Sagamu, run by the late schoolmaster and social reformer Tai Solarin." *You Must Set Forth At Dawn*, p. 377.)

753.   "Now they had to brave the forest and unpredictable border patrols in order to" what? ("In order to fly their time-ordered trade, gather at feasts of reunion, and celebrate their ancestral bonds. *You Must Set Forth At Dawn*, p. 389.)

754.   "However, forget that biblical promise 'Seek, and ye shall find,' I urged. This is a time to" what? ("To seek, but not to find." *You Must Set Forth At Dawn,* p. 401.)

755.   "Beneath my outward insouciance—this must be admitted—the contents of that journal" did what? ("Drilled corrosive hole into the most creative core of my being." *You Must Set Forth At Dawn,* p. 416.)

756.   "A year or so later, I would find myself setting up a meeting between the Irish Provos and the 'Regular.' Only one and third names have" what? ("Have stuck to my memory from that experience: Seamus Towney and, the one-third, Mac-something." *You Must Set Forth At Dawn,* p. 429.)

757.   "The response of the erstwhile fans, among others, was one cheering note, but a challenge also—it was a crop whose harvesting could not be long delayed, or it would shrivel in the heat of a tyrant's desperation." *You Must Set Forth At Dawn,* p. 445.)

758.   "I went straight from Temple Mount to" where? ("To the reception in the home of my host, and there a persistent journalist finally trapped and interviewed me on the usual themes, of which the immediate politics of Nigeria were prominent." *You Must Set Forth At Dawn,* p. 461.)

759.   "Julius handed over the document. Its conclusion could be summarized in" what? ("In two central demands and read as the defining statement of the opposition: a transitional government of national unity to take over from the military and,

simultaneously, the summoning of a sovereign national conference to debate and decide the future of the nation—its structure if it must continue as a federation, and its constitution." *You Must Set Forth At Dawn,* p. 475.)

760. "A despairing appeal for order: 'Listen, please! All of you, list to me! I want nobody to'" what? ("'To get hurt today, not at this homecoming. So please, stand aside, and let us move toward to car.'" *You Must Set Forth At Dawn,* p. 499.)

Poetry

XX. Idanre and other poems

761.   "Breaking earth upon a spring-haired elbow, lone a palm beyond" what? ("Beyond head-grains, spikes a guard of prim fronds, piercing high hairs of the wind." *Idandre and other Poems,* p. 9.)

762.   "Traveller you must set forth at dawn, I promise" what? ("I promise marvels of the holy hour." *Idandre and other Poems,* p. 11.)

763.   "Plague of comet tails, of bled horizons where egrets hone a sky-lane for" what? ("For worlds to turn on pennants." *Idandre and other Poems,* p. 13.)

764.   "In sounds as of the river's failing pulse, of shifting earth they make complaint. Grey presences of" what? ("Of head and hands who wander still adrift from understanding." *Idandre and other Poems,* p. 15.)

765.   "Higher than trees a cryptic crown Lord of the rebel three thorns lay" how? ("Lay asleep of down and myrrh; a mesh of mails, of flesh and words that flowered free." *Idandre and other Poems,* p. 17.)

766.   "Solemnly. Transfigures—the world" does what? ("The world spins on his spine, in still illusion." *Idandre and other Poems,* p. 19.)

767.   "Kinder these hard mangoes, greendrops at. The ear of" whom? ("At the ear of god-apparent,

coquettes to the future decadence." *Idandre and other Poems,* p. 21.)

768.   "Dolorous know please for me farm of hill" what? ("Please for me stream and wind take my voice." *Idandre and other Poems,* p. 23.)

769.   "As who would break earth, grief in" what? ("Grief in savage pounding, moulds her forehead where she kneels." *Idandre and other Poems,* p. 25.)

770.   "Seeking—as who has not? –beauty lodged" where? ("Beauty lodged in concaves of the yielded; conniving lies with self-encrimsoned mists." *Idandre and other Poems,* p. 27.)

771.   "Once and the repeated time, ageless though I puke, and when you" what? ("When you pour libations, each finger points me near the way I came." *Idandre and other Poems,* p. 29.)

772.   "There are more functions to a freezing plant than" what? ("Than stocking beer; cold biers of mortuaries submit their dues, harnessed—glory be!—" *Idandre and other Poems,* p. 31.)

773.   "Let me stammer my life down your endless lane the night is for" what? ("The night is for dreaming and a long bed of pain." *Idandre and other Poems,* p. 33.)

774.   "Her strength is wild, wild wild as the love that sings—this is" what? ("This is the last-born; giver me a joyful womb to bind." *Idandre and other Poems,* p. 35.)

775.   "You come as light rain not to quench but" what? ("But question out the pride of fire watchlight to my peace, within and out unguarded moments and the human hours." *Idandre and other Poems*, p. 37.)

776.   "Unleashed, exult. From wells deep in the brute's denials comes" what? ("Comes a captive tenderness." *Idandre and other Poems*, p. 39.)

777.   "The paradox of crowds set a marble wall where I fled for keeping. Loneliness feeds on open faces—once by" what? ("Once by little seeing, fell to the still centre, off the ruptured wheel." *Idandre and other Poems*, p. 41.)

778.   "I think it rains that tongues may" what? ("That tongues may loosen from the parch uncleave roof-tops of the mouth, hand heavy with knowledge." *Idandre and other Poems*, p. 43.)

779.   "Rust is ripeness, rust, and the wilted corn-plume; pollen is mating-time when" what? ("When swallows weave a dance of feathered arrows thread corn-stalks in winged streaks of light." *Idandre and other Poems*, p. 45.)

780.   "Too much pain, oh midwife at the cry of severance, fingers at "what? ("Fingers at the cosmic cord, too vast the pains of easters for a hint of the eternal." *Idandre and other Poems*, p. 47.)

781.   "Let nought be wasted, gather up for the recurrent session loaves of" what? ("Loaves of lead, lusting in the sun's recession." *Idandre and other Poems*, p. 49.)

782.　　"Shards of sunlight touch me here shredded in willows. Through stained-glass fragments on" what? ("On the lake I sought to reach a mind at silt-bed." *Idandre and other Poems,* p. 51.)

783.　　"You stood still for both eternities, and oh I heard the lesson of" what? ("I heard the lesson of your training sessions, cautioning—scorch earth behind you, do not leave a dubious neutral to the rear." *Idandre and other Poems,* p. 53.)

784.　　"Unsexed, your lips have framed a life curse shouting" what? ("Shouting joy where all the human world shared in grief's humility." *Idandre and other Poems,* p. 55.)

785.　　"So when the world grieves, rejoice call them to laughter, beat: what? ("Beat wilted welts on your breasts beat to hyenas of the wastes." *Idandre and other Poems,* p. 56.)

786.　　"In these white moments of my god, plucking light from the day's effacement, the last ember glows in" what? ("In his large creative hand, savage round the rebel mane, ribbed on ridges, crowded in corridors low on his spiked symbols." *Idandre and other Poems,* p. 61)

787.　　"And no one speaks of secrets in this land only, that the skin be" what? ("The skin be bared to welcome rain and earth prepare, that seeds may swell and roots take flesh within her, and men wake naked into harvest-tide." *Idandre and other Poems,* p. 62.)

788.　　"Calm, beyond interpreting, she sat and in her grace" did what? ("Shred wine with us. The quiet of the night shawled us together, secure she was in knowledge of that night's benediction. Ogun smiles his peace upon her, and we rose." *Idandre and other Poems,* p. 63.)

789.   "The silence yield to substance. They rose, the dead who fruit and oil await on doorstep shrine and road, their lips" what? ("Moist from the first flakes of harvest rain—even gods remember dues." *Idandre and other Poems,* p. 65.)

790.   "Later, diminutive zebras raced on track edges round the bed, dwarfs blew on royal bugles a gaunt ogboni raised" what? ("Raised his staff and vaulted on a zebra's back, galloped up a quivering nose—a battle with the suffocating shrouds." *Idandre and other Poems,* p. 67.)

791.   "Man's passage, pre-ordained, self-ordered winds in reconstruction. (Piecemeal was their deft re-birth, a cupped shell of tortoise, staggered tile tegument). And the monolith of man" does what? ("Searches still a blind hunger in the road's hidden belly." *Idandre and other Poems,* p. 69.)

792.   "His task was ended, he declined the crown of deities, sought retreat in heights. But Ire Laid skilled siege to divine withdrawal. Alas, for diplomatic arts, the Elders of Ire" die what? ("Prevailed; he descended, and they crowned him king." *Idandre and other Poems,* p. 71.)

793.   "We do not burn the woods to. trap" what? ("To trap a squirrel; we do not ask the mountain's aid, to crack a walnut." *Idandre and other Poems,* p. 73.)

794.   "This blade he forged, its progress never falters, rivulets on it so swift the blood" what? ("The blood forgets to clot." *Idandre and other Poems,* p. 75.)

795.   "The rodent's nose explored the shadows found sweat and gangrene smell the same to a skin tailor. Beyond a prayer for sunshine, what interest does" what? ("Does a stagnant pol pretend to a river in flood?" *Idandre and other Poems,* p. 77.)

796.   "Light filled me then, intruder thou I watched a god's excelsis; clearly the blasphemy of my humanity rose" how? ("Rose accusatory in my ears, and understanding came of a fatal condemnation." *Idandre and other Poems,* p. 79.)

797.   "I walked upon a deserted night before the gathering of Harvest, companion at a god's pre-banquet. The hills of Idanre: did what? ("Beckoned me as who would yield her secrets, locked in sepulchral granite." *Idandre and other Poems,* p. 81.)

798.   "Night sets me free; I suffer skies to sprout ebb to full navel in progressive arcs, ocean of a million roe highway of" what? ("Highway of eyes and moth-wings Night sets me free, I ride on ovary silences in the wake of ghosts." *Idandre and other Poems,* p. 83.)

799.   "Dawn, He who had dire reaped and in wrong season bade the forests" do what? ("Bade the forests swallow him and left mankind to harvest. At pilgrim lodge the wine-girl kept lone vigil, fused skill in her hour of charity." *Idandre and other Poems,* p. 84.)

800.   "And they moved towards resorption in His alloy essence primed to a fusion, primed to" what? ("To the sun's dispersion containment and communion, seed-time and harvest, palm and pylon, Ogun's road a 'Mobius' orbit, kernel and electrons, wine to alchemy." *Idandre and other Poems,* p. 85.)

XXI.   Mandela's Earth and other poems

801.   "Your logic frightens me, Mandela. Your logic frightens me. Those. Years of dreams, of time accelerated in visionary hopes, of" what? ("Of savoring the task anew, the call, the tempo primed to burst in supernovae round 'a brave new world'! Then stillness. Silence. The world closes round your role reality; the rest is…dreams." *Mandela's Earth and other Poems,* p. 3.)

802.   "Your patience grows inhuman, Mandela. Do you grow food? Do you make friends of" what? ("Of mice and lizards? Measures the grown of grass for time's unhurried pace?" *Mandela's Earth and other Poems,* p. 4.)

803.   "Your pulse, I know has slowed with "what? ("With earth's phlegmatic turns. I know your blood sagely warms and cools with seasons, responds to the lightest breeze yet scorns to race with winds (or hurricanes) that threaten change on tortoise pads." *Mandela's Earth and other Poems,* p. 5)

804.   "In your luxurious island home, outfitted state-of-the-art laboratory, ideas flow" where? ("Ideas flow out to pay the state in kind—protection for caste research, food for thought." *Mandela's Earth and other Poems,* p. 7.)

805.   "Rights of passage. Sheer sophistry! Skin is deep enough. Your lancet Mengele, was genius, creator hand so deft, made" what? ("Made anaesthetic optional—blue cornea graft, heart-liver swap, organic variants—eye in earhole, leg to armpit, brain transfer—all child's play. To you, but—not

even you could work a whole-skin graft. A thousand dead in the attempt makes proof enough—wouldn't you say?" *Mandela's Earth and other Poems,* p. 9.)

806.   "Ah yes, Mandela-Hess, you got us in this mess. The Allied Powers rightly hold. You pacing wall to wall, treading out" what? ("Treading out your grand designs in commie jackboots. Mandela-Mengele, you are ours! We'll keep you close." *Mandela's Earth and other Poems,* p. 10.)

807.   "So now they burn the roof above her head? Well, what's new? Retarded minds, like infants, play with fire. Bright things" do what? ("Bright things attract then. Color obsessed, did not these mewling agents once arrest your bedspread?" *Mandela's Earth and other Poems,* p. 11.)

808.   "A standard points the weary feet forward, yet" what? ("Yet wraps the hero's final stillness. This bedspread cushions us against the fall that absence makes." *Mandela's Earth and other Poems,* p. 12.)

809.   "No wonder the ad thus no need to curse the futile rage, the puny stabs of flames disfiguring the night. Death twitches: what? ("Death. Twitches these centuries' buried minds in misinformation." *Mandela's Earth and other Poems,* p. 13.)

810.   "How could they know, these living dead the flames their fumbling hands have fanned, inscribe" what? ("Inscribe the very colors they proscribe across our darkest nights," *Mandela's Earth and other Poems,* p. 14.)

811.   "We wish to bury our dead. Now, a funeral is a many-cultured thing. Some races would rope a heifer to" what? ("To the slaughter stone, or goat/ram/pig or humble cockerel, monochrome or striped, spotted, seamless—the soothsayer rules the aesthetics or rank and circumstance of the dear deceased." *Mandela's Earth and other Poems,* p. 15.)

812.   "O dearly beloved, we wish to mourn. But first, shall we lance some ancient tumuli? Probe" what? ("Probe some birthly portents, glorified demise?" *Mandela's Earth and other Poems,* p. 16.)

813.   "We wish to bury our dead. Others boast horsemen sentinels, ranged in Chinese Catacombs, silent guards on" what? ("On vanished dynasties. Or their Nilotic counterparts—did time stand still for these?" *Mandela's Earth and other Poems,* p. 17.)

814.   "We wish to bury our dead. Let all take note, our dead were" what? ("Our dead were none of these eternal hoarders—does the buyer of nothing seek after-sales service?" *Mandela's Earth and other Poems,* p. 18.)

815.   "We wished to bury our dead, we rendered unto Caesar what was Caesar's. The right to" what? ("The right. To congregate approved; hold procession, eulogize, lament procured for a standard fee. All death tariff settled in advance, receipted, logged." *Mandela's Earth and other Poems,* p. 19.)

816.   "Sea urchins stung his soul. Albino eels searched the cortex of his heart, his hands thrust" where? ("His hands thrust high to exorcise visions of

lost years, slow parade of isolation's ghosts."
Mandela's Earth and other Poems, p. 21.)

817.   "No! I am no prisoner of this rock, this island,
no ash spew on Milky Ways to" what? ("To
conquests old or new. I am this rock, this island. I
toiled, precedent on this soil, as in the great dark
whale of time, Black Hole of the galaxy." *Mandela's
Earth and other Poems,* p. 23.)

818.   "An old man of sixty-five ekes out his life in
prison sops. The poet strings you" what? ("The poet
strings you these lines, Mandela, to stay from
stringing lead." *Mandela's Earth and other Poems,*
p. 25.)

819.   Once, for a dare he filled his heart-shaped
swimming pool with" what? ("With bank notes, high
denomination and fed a pound of caviar to his dog.
The dog was sick; a chartered plane flew in
replacement for the Persian rug." *Mandela's Earth
and other Poems,* p. 29.)

820.   "Water is a god that does its favors by the
drop, and" what? ("And waiting is a way of life.
Rebellion gleamed yet faintly in his eye traversing
chrome-and-platinum retreats." *Mandela's Earth
and other Poems,* p. 30.)

821.   "Not she dispensed, but took the coated pill.
Cleopatra's needle feel from" what? ("From hands
incontinent while Caesar's feet stamped patterns of
his will on outspread rugs of an enchanted
continent." *Mandela's Earth and other Poems,* p.
31.)

822.   "To mask the real, the world is turned a stage, a rampant play of" what? ("A rampant play of symbols masks a people's rage." *Mandela's Earth and other Poems,* p. 33.)

823.   "Till the people's fiesta: a blood-red streamer in Monrovian skies, a lamppost and" what? ("And— the swinging Redeemer." *Mandela's Earth and other Poems,* p. 34.)

824.   "Grim passages predict an amphitheater of deadly games, of rites of menace. A lion prowls beyond to" what? ("A lion prowls beyond to feed these Romans' lust." *Mandela's Earth and other Poems,* p. 37.)

825.   "I too have dared (and fled) the rage of those primordial capsules, range of motion through "what? ("Through Manhattan's bowels, Bronx and Brooklyn, Harlem, Queens, rodeo tumbrils plying shallow routes through Mammon's sated belly." *Mandela's Earth and other Poems,* p. 39.)

826.   "A sublime encounter without precedent? The less time needed to regurgitate" what? ("The mush of instant commentary." *Mandela's Earth and other Poems,* p. 41.)

827.   "Mind calloused to universal loss, our man declined to" what? ("Declined to blink, stayed squarely on the ball. The ghoulish game began." *Mandela's Earth and other Poems,* p. 43.)

828.   "A vagrant curses off" what? ("The lingering fumes of last night's laced methyl. Trash cans are milestones of his quest, the inns and fields of leisured

foraging. Contempt replies the stares." *Mandela's Earth and other Poems*, p. 45.)

829.   "The camera flees distressed. But not before" what? ("Not before the fire of battle flashes in. those eyes rekindled by the moment's urge to center stage." *Mandela's Earth and other Poems*, p. 47.)

830.   "Yet no one sees his face, he waits for" what? ("For no reply, only that. Combination three-four calling card, the wasp-tail legend: I've been here and gone." *Mandela's Earth and other Poems*, p. 49.)

831.   "Multinaira clinics raised to heal. The shelves stare empty, surgery pans are" what? ("Are rusted. The doctor's reassuring smile replaces drugs, his hand prescribes placebos, crosses off the hopeless case and saves the last pill for a worthier soul." *Mandela's Earth and other Poems*, p. 51.)

832.   "Police checkpoint: 'I could shoot you now,' the lawman screams, and" what? ("And pulls the trigger. An athlete's brains disperse the pleas of Good Samaritans. Peacemakers dodge gray flakes on motor chassis, paste on arid tar." *Mandela's Earth and other Poems*, p. 53.)

833.   "Since justice is but One, it must be seized not piecemeal but entire, or not at all, and pleas for the moment's justice shall" what? ("Shall not be. No more defiant streams of spittle, no, not from enfeebled throats whose desperation douses arsonists' flames, for these are not." *Mandela's Earth and other Poems*, p. 55.)

834.   "Stirring in your yellowing scroll of ivory slogans. They scream: You'll not" what? ("You'll not emboss my shroud in slogans! But if phrasemongers have indeed usurped the word, and dreams come packaged, handy like a sausage roll, the poet chooses; DANGER—DREAMS AT WORK. Now mark my slogan well." *Mandela's Earth and other Poems,* p. 56.)

835.   "So when I offer me, a medium as" what? ("As the windowpane, you beat upon it frantic wings against unyielding tolerance?" *Mandela's Earth and other Poems,* p. 59.)

836.   "When Ogun slammed his anvil down the flinty earth of Idanre, its shock waves burrowed" where? ("Its shock waves burrowed through millennia, surfaced in charged outcrops, sinuous offsprings, seven-ridged rockhills of Ile-Ife." *Mandela's Earth and other Poems,* p. 61.)

837.   "Peace, peace, acquisitor heart. Still your pangs of greed ,quit longing, douse hunger. Shun" what? ("Shun furtive middlemen assailing Christian, Muslim convertites, ministers to aesthetic lust— 'Bring out your forsaken gods; this agent serves paymasters for apostasy.'" *Mandela's Earth and other Poems,* p. 63.)

838.   "The mind attunes to loss—a mercy death. To save the grove, we isolate the three; beyond" what? ("Beyond all cure, uproot, incinerate." *Mandela's Earth and other Poems,* p. 65.)

839.   "The cinders of past epochs sink—but slowly. Lack of substance clings" how?

("Tenaciously to form. Pillars rise in flames of conquest, peel, incandescent. The reel unwinds in timeless cycles: a spearpoint's taper of light." *Mandela's Earth and other Poems,* p. 67.)

840.   "Alas, what's gone is gone. The rain affirms the loss. Grace that was a fiery dying congeals. The skies have opened, gods and hero-gods blot" what? ("Blot all traces of their erstwhile dance with mortals, uphold the lore of pinpricks mere woodworms may pronounce on golden realms." *Mandela's Earth and other Poems,* pp. 69-70.)

XXII. Samarkand and Other Markets I Have Known

841.   "I shall ram pebbles in my mouth Demosthenes not to choke, but" what? ("But half dolphin, half shark hammerhead from fathoms deep ride the waves to charge the breakers they erect, crush impediments of power and inundate their tainted towers—I shall ram pebbles in my mouth." *Samarkand and Other Markets I Have Known,* p. 3.)

842.   "In swarms as locusts, as lies and flies, consorts drawn to dark orgies of commemorating pens—long is the line of" what? ("Long is the line of great deductions lure of east within our chequered tribe—from griots of voice, to plume, and the compact processor." *Samarkand and Other Markets I Have Known,* p. 5.)

843.   "Why lament? Is it lost time? Days irretrievable? Why play the cards of time with "what? ("With vain resentment and thus augment the deficit imposed by usurper hands in stolen spaces?" *Samarkand and Other Markets I Have Known,* p. 7.)

844.   "Why ponder the lost hours, and years? We know which way they flew, what leeches—native only for" what? ("Native only for the soil that suckled the –sank sly proboscis deep in open veins and piped our life blood through indifferent seas." *Samarkand and Other Markets I Have Known,* p. 9.)

845.   "Does she feel eyes, and shuffling feet and swiveling heads, arrest Martinis Midway to genteel throats? She does not" what? ("She does not fidget. No Morse code filters through her feet cases in soft-

leather ease, to read impatience." *Samarkand and Other Markets I Have Known,* p. 11.)

846.   "Then came the love affair. A tease, a foreplay a realignment of limbs and mock passes with" what? ("With steel nutcrackers over prostrate yet aggressive curvatures. When it came, the crunch was massive—as the silence drawn in turned heads and suspended gestures. Eyes turned to floundering fish." *Samarkand and Other Markets I Have Known,* p. 12.)

847.   "It was an afternoon of indifferent news the world was still, the world was turbid. I had great need of" what? ("Of a universe that still was peopled, lived, loved and died, ate and defecated, wrapped its legs around a table stem." *Samarkand and Other Markets I Have Known,* p. 13.)

848.   "His sign is terminal, he tells the poet what other clinics had long diagnosed—short-sighted in one eye" and what? ("And long I the other. The patients waits, the explosion comes on cue—'but not within the limits we call nature! A little difference that's the norm but this" These, sir belong to different pairs of eyes!'" *Samarkand and Other Markets I Have Known,* p. 15.)

849.   "The buzzer from front desk recalls him to his waiting patients. His shoulders sag. 'Come back tomorrow. I may'" what? ("'I may summon aa second opinion. The receptionist will find a vacant slot. I hope. One slot? Best make it three. Or five. Maybe we should allot one entire morning to your cases. Yes, a second opinion. Two heads are better

than one.'" *Samarkand and Other Markets I Have Known,* p. 16.)

850.   "Death touches all, both kin and strangers. The death of one, we know, is" what? ("Is one death too many. Grief unites, but grief's manipulation thrusts our worlds apart in more than measurable distances—there are tears of cultured pearls, while others drop as silent stones." *Samarkand and Other Markets I Have Known,* p. 19.)

851.   "Long, long before he slipped Viagra down his throat, and" what? ("And washed it down with 3-Barrl rotgut, his favourite gargle from Iganmu, libeled home-made brandy as in home-made democracy, the Gunner was a goner." *Samarkand and Other Markets I Have Known,* p. 21.)

852.   "A blindfold, wider than nations and more craved stretched, it seemed" where? ("Across spires and domes, cross and crescent, tones in the golden haze of dusk, snaked through bronze warrens, spice and leather alleys, date trestles, sandalwood, olive groves and sparse oases, wound through catacombs where piety preys and wounds." *Samarkand and Other Markets I Have Known,* p. 23.)

853.   "All that could be done waw done, the best of skills exhausted, no limits placed on" what? ("On what the purse could buy. The rest was vanity. He called the learned to his side to debate mortality." *Samarkand and Other Markets I Have Known,* p. 25.)

854.   "The Party of the Niger Delta rules by the barrel—oil and gun—a marriage made in heaven.

Market forces write the law, rigs and derricks scorch" what? ("Scorch the landscape, livelihood and lives. Marionettes in itchy uniforms salute and settle civil strife on 'orders from above'—the only tongue they learn—for oil must flow through land and sea though both be silted from contempt and greed." *Samarkand and Other Markets I Have Known,* p. 27.)

855.　　"I never really knew you. I cling to yours because I own" what? ("I own a closer death, a death that dared elude prophetic sight. Dreams we all share, but" what? ("But close presentiment, may hover round the head, invisible to all it most concerns. We had become immune to dread." *Samarkand and Other Markets I Have Known,* p. 29.)

856.　　"I. think sometimes of poems I have lost— maybe their loss it was that saved the world—still they do get lost, and" what? ("And I recall them only when a fragment levitates behind discarded invoices." *Samarkand and Other Markets I Have Known,* p. 33.)

857.　　"I think of voices I have lost, and touches, the fleeting brush" of what? ("Of eyes that burrows deep within the heart of need, the pledge unspoken, the more than acts of faith that forge an instant world in silent pact with strangers—deeper, deeper bonds than the dearest love's embrace." *Samarkand and Other Markets I Have Known,* p. 34.)

858.　　"Departures linger. Absences do not deplete the tavern. They hang over "what? ("They hang over the haze as exhalations from receded shores. Soon, night repossess the silence, but till dawn the notes hold sway, smokey epiphanies, possessive of the hours." *Samarkand and Other Markets I Have Known,* p. 35.)

859.   "His eyes turn lamps on the chamber of a chrysalis stuck to leaf or twig, dangling from died mucilage. He knows its history this renewed pulsation triumphant egress, clammy I "what? ("In birds fluids, flapping dry then liftin on furry, variegated wings." *Samarkand and Other Markets I Have Known,* p. 37.)

860.   "Those eyes grow deeper with the years, grow into" what? ("Into seasons of glut and drought, frenzy and repose." *Samarkand and Other Markets I Have Known,* p. 38.)

861.   "He wakes from a prolonged delirium, swears he has seen" what? ("The face of God. God help all those whose fever never raged or has subsided." *Samarkand and Other Markets I Have Known,* p. 43.)

862.   "They would be killers anyway, and anywhere. Their world's a hiatus. Jerked to life, they suck" what? ("The teats of piety, briefly shed a long cocoon of death. Death eyes, a death humility, death wish, dead end a death asymmetry that befits a death-bound unbeginning." *Samarkand and Other Markets I Have Known,* p. 44.)

863.   "A god is nowhere born, yet everywhere,. But Rama's sect rejects" what? ("That fine distinction—the designated spot is sanctified, not for piety but—for dissolution of yours from mine, politics of hate—and forced exchange—peace for a

moment's ecstasy." *Samarkand and Other Markets I Have Known,* p. 45.)

864.   "Some words are coarse, indecent. They make a case for" what? ("For censorship, such words as pagan, heathen, infidel, unbeliever, kafiri, etc. The cleric swears he'll sweep the streets clean of the unclean, armed with Book and Beard." *Samarkand and Other Markets I Have Known,* p. 47.)

865.   "A market is kind haven for the wandering soul or the merely ruminant. Each stall is shrine and temple, magic cave of" what? ("Magic cave or memorabilia. Its passages are grottoes that transport us, bargain hunters all, from pole to antipodes, annulling time, evoking places and host histories." *Samarkand and Other Markets I Have Known,* p. 49.)

866.   "Still, here and there, one lashes out—recall the prince of peace turned" what? ("Turned manic in a synagogue turned market place?" *Samarkand and Other Markets I Have Known,* p. 51.)

867.   "So much for ancient times—today the strings are muted. Samarkand's sibling markets on these continents have" what? ("Have fallen to dry dirges, dropped to thin laments beneath collapsing thatch." *Samarkand and Other Markets I Have Known,* p. 53.)

868.   "I spurn this double counterfeit—wages earned in goods from plant assemblage—brassieres, jars of mayonnaise, jockstraps, plated cutlery" and what? ("Diapers, negligees and curtain rods, shaving cream, deodorants, tourist wares, the ever-replicating

babushka…where barter is debased, and leisure must be shared in after hours converted wages-merchandise to a common currency devalued from the source." *Samarkand and Other Markets I Have Known,* p. 55.)

869.   "The marketplace of hate is quartered on the pious tongue but this old man knew" what? ("Knew yet kept his daily tryst with haggling cries, mock wars of merchandise mint tea and gossip, an avocation to observe and chronicle." *Samarkand and Other Markets I Have Known,* p. 57.)

870.   "One market day, in the souk of Cairo, the zealot's counterfeiting hand did" what? ("Did not triumph. The moving finger writes, and having writ…the mind survives to sing the way on the Golden Road where drams of Samarkand outlive tomorrow's market. Day." *Samarkand and Other Markets I Have Known,* p. 59)

871.   "The children of this land are old. Their eyes are fixed on maps in place of land. Their feet must" what? ("Must learn to follow distant contours. Traced by alien minds. Their present sense has faded into past." *Samarkand and Other Markets I Have Known,* p. 63.)

872.   "A new race will supersede the present—where love is" what? ("Where love is banished stranger, lonely wanderer in forests prowled by lust, on feral pads of power." *Samarkand and Other Markets I Have Known,* p. 64.)

873.   "Should it matter that the tower clock no longer tells the time, its hands arrested like" what?

("Like the hands of God in mid-creation? Whose dare is this that seals all faces of the compassed spire in ponderous slabs of bronze." *Samarkand and Other Markets I Have Known,* p. 65.)

874.   "Wrapped in flirtatious blades of grass, you'll find them, derelict sentinels, where lizards conduct" what? ("Their blatant rapes, metronomic heads ablaze. These are the planners' masterpieces—shelter for all by the new millennium—low-cost housing schemes, lowly and costly—long on invoices and short on shelter..." *Samarkand and Other Markets I Have Known,* p. 67.)

875.   "To drums of ancient skins, homeopathic beat against the boom of pale-knuckled guns. We vied with" what? ("With the regal rectitude of Overamwen—no stranger. Breath—he swore—shall desecrate this hour of communion with our gods!" *Samarkand and Other Markets I Have Known,* p. 69.)

876.   "Alas for lost idylls. Like Levi jeans on youth and age, the dreams are faded, potholed at" what? ("At joints and even milder points of stress." *Samarkand and Other Markets I Have Known,* p. 71.)

877.   "Chime much louder than the flutes of poets, their sirens lure the bravest to their doom. But some survive, and survival breeds" what? ("Survival breeds, it seems, unending debts. Time is our usurer, but earth remains sole signatory to life's covenant—and thus I ask: whose feet are these upon the storehouse loft?" *Samarkand and Other Markets I Have Known,* p. 73.)

878.　　　"We who neither curse their gods nor desecrate their texts, their prayer mats or altars—what shall we do, Chinua, with "what? ("With these hate clerics? While we sleep, their fingers spread as brambles, deface our Book of Life." *Samarkand and Other Markets I Have Known,* p. 75.)

879.　　　"The masquerade's falsetto may reveal "what? ("Not artifice but loss of voice, its gutturals camouflage death throes, not echoes of our spirit realms." *Samarkand and Other Markets I Have Known,* p. 77.)

880.　　　"We, the children of disdain, infidels of earth when we seek—like they—our turn upon the throne of justice, let that mantra be" what? ("Be now silenced that has feigned till now—the end shall justify. The means—and allied canticles. Let our shrines and wished-for palaces be not founded yet again upon the peace of innocence. Let not evil call to evil in a ring of time's entrapment, a wheel of fire and blood whose spinning will consume at will." *Samarkand and Other Markets I Have Known,* p. 79.)

Essays

XXIII. InterInventions: Between Defective Memory and the Public Lie

881.   "For me, I respect an honest and truthful peasant more than" what? ("More than I respect a deceitful and lying president. I was brought up to know and to believe that lying is the beginning of almost all crimes and sins. I was trained In the classic military mould as an officer and gentleman who can be taken on his word. A liar will invariably be a fraud, a rogue, a murderer. I say like David 'I abhor the assembly of evildoers and refuse to sit with the wicked. Compromise with evil is both evil and sinful.'" *InterInventions: Between Defective Memory and the Public Lie,* p.)

882.   "To settle the question nof absence of malice beyond all doubt, we are. Both "what? ("We are both wine-lovers, and right n ow, my only outstanding grudge against him is that he is still hoarding a vintage Mouton Rothschild—a birthday gift from his overseas partners—that I thought we were supposed to have demolished at least a year ago at a specially organized private session." *InterInventions: Between Defective Memory and the Public Lie,* p. 11.)

883.   "A special category of public falsifications— such has been my distressing observation—has to do with" what? ("With one's relationships—real or imagined, craved or feared—with power." *InterInventions: Between Defective Memory and the Public Lie,* p. 20.)

884.   "That lonesome success of titular emulation attests to my belief that at least one viable work may emerge even from" what? ("Even from a pedestrian mind trapped in a parochial groove. That truism holds, not only for polemical tracts, but for fiction." *InterInventions: Between Defective Memory and the Public Lie,* p. 29.)

885.   "He is now—supposedly—grownup. It is a time to remind him" what? ("That the stern rod of Ogun awaits all lying tongues." *InterInventions: Between Defective Memory and the Public Lie,* p. 38.)

886.   Als, Ibrahim was very much preoccupied with" what? ("With restoring trust between us when a bizarre combination of circumstances resulted in my believing that he tried to hunt me down in Makurdi' Audu Ogbeh's home, when I went hunting on my own during a conference of ANA, the Association of Nigerian Authors." *InterInventions: Between Defective Memory and the Public Lie,* p. 47.)

887.   "Murder—or assassination—as a literary theme, has always provided" what? ("Riveting, or simply escapist reading for the human mind—mediocre, average, sophisticated, etc." *Inter-Inventions: Between Defective Memory and the Public Lie,* p. 56.)

888.   "Could he possibly have mistaken the Christiah exhortation—'Watch and Pray' for" what? ("For his private inclination to 'Watch and Prey'?" *InterInventions: Between Defective Memory and the Public Lie,* p. 65.)

889.   "This recidivist Salawu, on that same Judgment Day—as the lawyers on both sides plus" what? ("Plus the audience at the final act of the court would testify, did everything to cadge a photo-op of us together outside the court premises, with sudden sorties that tested my dodging skills to the limit." *InterInventions: Between Defective Memory and the Public Lie,* p. 74.)

890.   "The criminal courts however must be answered, and" what? ("And there we shall leave Gbenda Daniel to attend to his charges of corruption." *InterInventions: Between Defective Memory and the Public Lie,* p. 83.)

891.   "I had waived any monetary recompense, demanded only" what? ("Only a symbolic fine of One Naira in settlement and of course publication of his retraction and apology in the media." *InterInventions: Between Defective Memory and the Public Lie,* p. 92.)

892.   "He pleaded that his offence at the OYRSC was minor, that he had" what? ("That he had endured public humiliation and made to refund the misappropriated amount." *InterInventions: Between Defective Memory and the Public Lie,* p. 101.)

893.   "On that occasion, Salawu not only wrote petitions, he" what? ("He placed an advertisement in the newspapers to withdraw his earlier public apology made more than six months before. His action was a contempt of the court and judiciary but we simply chose to ignore him." *InterInventions: Between Defective Memory and the Public Lie,* p. 110.)

894.	"It is important that this nation, and the entire world of culture and ethical pursuit understand" what? ("No court judgment exists that voids a single provision of this law—including the setting up of a new board—or its entirety." *InterInventions: Between Defective Memory and the Public Lie,* p. 119.)

895.	"Ultimately, the lawyers will have their day in court, and the Law will have a final say. Until then, however" what? ("The legitimate CBCIU, acting as an entity, or simply as individuals and citizens, will continued to educate the public on the ethical implications of seemingly public spirited ventures, and frustrate efforts by any party to extend the purlieu of fraudulent activities that drag that name—and the nation—down to an undeserved level of international regard." *InterInventions: Between Defective Memory and the Public Lie,* p. 129.)

XXIV. Myth, Literature and the African World

896.   "I shall begin by commemorating the gods for" what? ("For their self-sacrifice on the altar of literature, and in so doing press them into further service on behalf of human society, and its quest for the explication of being." *Myth, Literature and the African World*, p. 1.)

897.   "He is brought under control only by Oxala, the victim of the original injustice, who" what? ("Who rebukes Sango's blasphemy." *Myth, Literature and the African World*, p. 9)

898.   "There are, of course, a few points to quarrel with in that the concept of expiating a racial burden is" what? ("Is something which has been taken over from Judeo-Christianity. Compensation and restitution are natural enough goals for an enslaved race in those circumstances, but expiation of a racial burden is pure racial transposition by the guilty." *Myth, Literature and the African World*, p. 17.)

899.   "In plays from the original source the gods are conceived more in the imagery of" what? ("Of peat, chalk, oil, kernels, blood, heartwood and tuber, and active metaphors of human social preoccupations." *Myth, Literature and the African World*, p. 25.)

900.   "We shall leave the latter Marxist speculations alone, as" what? ("As being outside the scope of this subject." *Myth, Literature and the African World*, p. 33.)

901.   "Ritual theatre, let. It be recalled, establishes" what? ("The spatial medium not merely as a physical area for simulated events but as a manageable contraction of the cosmic envelop within which man—no matter how deeply buried such a consciousness has latterly become—fearfully exists." *Myth, Literature and the African World,* p. 41.)

902.   "And the most significant discovery, or more accurately, recognition is that we encounter in such plays a complete, hermetic universe of forces or being. This is" what? ("This is the most fundamental attribute of all true tragedy, no matter where geographically placed." *Myth, Literature and the African World,* p. 49.)

903.   "Tragic dram of this nature (and tragic poetry) operates through" what? ("Operates through the homoeopathic principle, and it should cause no surprise to find the expression 'praise-song' applied to such wanton savagery, or. To find in performance that the lines are changed with a non-critical, adulatory and joyous involvement." *Myth, Literature and the African World,* p. 57.)

904.   "It will be necessary also to suspend our habitual prejudices in our approach to this literature. The expression 'social vision' is chosen as" what? ("As a convenient delimitation for certain types of literature to be discussed, not as an elevated concept of the type." *Myth, Literature and the African World,* p. 65.)

905.   "The play offers a mordant dissection of a specialized category of the same racial situation and

188

reveals" what? ("In a more subtle and effective way some thread of hope for the breakdown of racial barriers." *Myth, Literature and the African World,* p. 73.)

906.   "This, let it be remembered, was at least forty years before" what? ("Before the tentative efforts of the Vatican to effect a reconciliation, not of course with non-Christian religions, but with the various pieces which broke away when the Rock of St Peter began to crack." *Myth, Literature and the African World,* p. 79.)

907.   "Whatever emerges triumphant? This orientation of emphasis towards the metaphor of contest is" what? ("Is by no means comprehensive, but it is inevitable from the point of view of our overall theme." *Myth, Literature and the African World,* p. 85.)

908.   "Yet this priest aspires to no less than cosmic control. The six villages, as a result of an unfruitful consultation, would be" what? ("Would be locked in the old year for two moons longer." *Myth, Literature and the African World,* p. 91.)

909.   "Africa minus the Sahara North is still a very large continent, populated by" what? ("By myriad races and cultures. With its millions of inhabitants it must be the largest metaphysical vacuum ever conjured up for the purpose of racist propaganda." *Myth, Literature and the African World,* p. 97.)

910.   "How ironic that the novel's only episode of consciously rendered affectionate relationship should be" what? (Should be homosexual, and yet

how appropriate to Oulouguem's misanthropic vision." *Myth, Literature and the African World,* p. 103.)

911.   "The long ignominious silence of African leaders over the now resolved Anyanya insurrection in the Sudan, is" what? ("Alas, the misleading yardstick by which the majority judge the truth of such expression of the authentic will to identity. Missing always is that tempter of comprehension which recognizes in the various adaptive modes of expression aspects of the same crucial struggle for a re-statement of self and society." *Myth, Literature and the African World,* p. 109,)

912.   "We do not utter praise of arms. The praise of arms is the praise of things, and what shall we all the soul crawling so low, soul so" what? ("Soul so hollow it finds fulfillment in the praising of mere things?" *Myth, Literature and the African World,* p. 115.)

913.   "The realities of this African world are by no means deodorized, though the language of mundane trivia often" what? ("Often acquires hints of mystical import." *Myth, Literature and the African World,* p. 124.)

914.   "Negritude is the low ebb in a dialectical progression. The theoretical and practical assertion of white supremacy is the thesis; negritude's roles as" what? ("As an antithetical value is the negative stage." *Myth, Literature and the African World,* p. 134.)

915.   "Tragedy, in Yoruba traditional drama, is the anguish of this severance, the fragmentation of essence from" what? ("The fragmentation of essence from self. Its music is the stricken cry of man's blind soul as he flounders in the void and crashes through a deep abyss of spirituality and cosmic rejection." *Myth, Literature and the African World,* p. 145.)

XXV. The Burden of Memory the Muse of Forgiveness

916.   "Was the mission of Mr Duke in South Africa by any chance to promote the cause of South Africa's Truth and Reconciliation Commission?" ("No. Very much the contrary. Duke was visiting that country to express solidarity with a self-declared independent Free Boer Republic—inspired perhaps by the American Freemen enclave?—which had resolved that apartheid may be officially outlawed in the new South Africa but its extreme right-wing members, densely located in a town royally named Balmoral, had different ideas of what the relationship between races should be." *The Burden of Memory,* p. 5.)

917.   "Other commissions make no claims beyond setting out the facts, a procedure that, in the main, grants no immunity beforehand (or very rarely, as a version of 'plea bargaining') and" what? ("And does not foreclose the many possible mechanisms of some form of restitution by the inculpated." *The Burden of Memory,* p. 15.)

918.   "A collective levy need not be regarded as" what? ("As a punitive measure; indeed—since the purpose is reconciliation, such an offer could originate from the beneficiaries of Apartheid themselves, in a voluntary. Gesture of atonement—it need not be a project of the state." *The Burden of Memory,* p. 25.)

919.   "And here, I believe, is where the cry for Reparations for a different and more ancient cause suggests" what? ("Suggests itself as the missing link

between Truth and Reconciliation." *The Burden of Memory,* p. 35.)

920.   "Now that provokes a number of ethical issues. There has to be" what? ("There has to be a moral foundation to all quests for equity—he who comes to the court of equity, says the Latin proverb, just approach with clean hands." *The Burden of Memory,* p. 45.)

921.   "It simply seems to me rather presumptuous to offer absolution to" whom? ("To the practitioner of a dehumanizing trade through an exercise in comparative degrees of abuse." *The Burden of Memory,* p. 55.)

922.   "Of all the landmarks of slavery that I had ever traversed, none, not even the grim tunnels of Goree of Cape Coast, worn smooth by the yet echoing slaps of feet on the passage into hell, could match" what? ("Could match the eerie evocation no f the walk toward Embarkation Point on the coast of Ouiday, in the Republic of Benin, then known as the Kingdom of Dahomey." *The Burden of Memory,* p. 65.)

923.   "There is an ongoing context to such innovative tendencies and it is" what? ("It is a context that constitutes its own worrisome critique. Or, let. Us put this differently, and with a more cogent summons, are certain n aspects of these proceedings not in. themselves a tarnishing of the quality of Truth and its imperatives and, thus, a condonation of impunity." *The Burden of Memory,* p. 75.)

924.   "The obvious response to this is that it was not governments that were enslaved in the first place, but peoples, and" what? ("And the peoples are far more sinned against (and by their own rulers past and present) than sinning." *The Burden of Memory,* p. 85.)

925.   "It had a rather wistful, valedictory tone in the circumstances, resurrecting, in one of those strange flashbacks, a long receded image—straight from" what? ("Straight from my student days: a frail figure by a staircase, an operatic baritone singing *Guten Abend* during a Christmas telecast—just one of those instant flashes that superimpose themselves on an actuality." *The Burden of Memory,* p. 95.)

926.   "Such lines, like the rejection of differentiation, the humane empathy in the works of the cited war poets, do not" what? ("Do not, however, glorify the enemy, only portray them as comrades caught in the vice of a universal irrationality." *The Burden of Memory,* p. 115.)

927.   "Dominating the entire corpus of Negritude literature, however, was, inevitably" what? ("The direction of the subject itself—where should it head? And the divisions were not along the boundaries of language, but of vision and both creative and intellectual temperament." *The Burden of Memory,* p. 135.)

928.   "Language, therefore, it does appear, is" what? ("Is not everything, and we may bear this in mind in attempting to place emphasis on the peculiar circumstances that made the Francophone writer respond to the colonial experience through literary

tools and an artistic movement, unlike his Anglophone counterpart." *The Burden of Memory,* p. 155.)

929.   "My summation remains the same, however, and Maunick proceeds to identify with—as indicated in that last line—and react. To the political plight or adventure of the community of race. When you share identity with 'the wretched of the earth,' other identities take" what? ("Take second place or appear comparatively academic." *The Burden of Memory,* p. 175.)

930.   "Within such a context, the Sosso-Bala becomes" what? ("An unsolicited metaphor for the near intolerable burden of memory, a Muse for the poetry of identity and that elusive 'leaven' in the dough of humanity—forgiveness, the remission of wrongs, and a recovery of lost innocence." *The Burden of Memory,* p. 194.)

XXVI. The Open Sore of a Continent: A personal Narrative of the Nigerian Crisis

931.   "One ongoing actuality of repression very easily obscures another; it is" what? ("It is a familiar and understandable pattern, one that dictatorships, especially of the most. Cynical kind, exploit most effectively." *The Open Sore of a Continent,* p. 4.)

932.   "These voices, however, and the history that brought then into being, and with such resolve, have" what? ("Have already ensured that Abacha is the last despot who will impose himself on the Nigerian nation." *The Open Sore of a Continent,* p. 15.)

933.   "If you reexamine the various properties that we have listed as being germane to the definition of a state (and I use that word loosely) we may find" what? ("That the so-called tribal kingdoms or clan principalities that were later supplanted by European imperialist arrangements do indeed qualify for nation status." *The Open Sore of a Continent,* p. 25.)

934.   "On our part, it is sufficient to state—not even to explain but simply to declare" what? ("Our preference for continuing as one nation." *The Open Sore of a Continent,* p. 35.)

935.   "The Biafran and Ojukwu's grip on the world's historical memory is so deep that even today, and indeed during any post-Biafran crisis, I find" what? ("I am often asked this question: By the way, what has become of that Biafran man, you know, the one with the heavy beard and heavier Oxford accent?" *The Open Sore of a Continent,* p. 45.)

936. "We were confronted, still are, by a dictatorship specimen that was unprecedented in our experience of military viciousness. Under Abacha's direct command" what happened? ("Over two hundred peaceful demonstrators had been mown down in cold blood on the streets of Lagos." *The Open Sore of a Continent*, p. 55.)

937. "More to the point, for now, he also turned Nigeria into" what? ("Into a police state as the countdown toward the 1983 election began in earnest, and he found himself compelled to read the cheerless writing on the wall." *The Open Sore of a Continent*, p. 65.)

938. "By the 1983 election, most. Of the avenues for siphoning money from government coffers had" what? (Had become atrophied for lack of content at the source." *The Open Sore of a Continent*, p. 75.)

939. "Nothing therefore would satisfy this bilious duo until "what? ("Until the old man was publicly tarred with the brush of corruption." *The Open Sore of a Continent*, p. 85.)

940. "The answer to that is twofold. First, Umarus Dikko had" what? ("Had gone even further than Babatope. His was not simply a matter of deductive prophesying; he had prior knowledge of Buhari's coup and had warned Shehu Shagari about the plot." *The Open Sore of a Continent*, p. 95.)

941. "The triumph of his treacherous colleagues in that 1983 election was" what? ("Was to be short-lived, however, as a few months into the renewed mandate of Shehu Shagari, the military struck, and

Buhari and Ibiagbon unleased their own brand of terrorism on the nation." *The Open Sore of a Continent,* pp. 105-106.)

942.   "That bedrock has not budged and its adherents have" what? ("Have clung to it like limpets, defying the direction-changing storms of ideological imperatives." *The Open Sore of a Continent,* p. 115.)

943.   "Hunger stalks the streets and, with it, desperation. Thus, security of individuals has" what? ("Has become a game of Russian roulette; one never knows whose turn it is." *The Open Sore of a Continent,* p. 125.)

944.   "However, our guiding representatives of governments do continue to agree with us, the alienated, nation-denigrating, brainwashed Westerners negativists, and" who? ("And professional doom-sayers, whose sense of sophistication is simply to pull down their own peoples before Western eyes and so on and so forth." *The Open Sore of a Continent,* p. 135.)

945.   "What sort of nation is this? We grasp only too painfully what the nation can be, what it deserves to be. If Ken Saro-Wiwa's death-cry does prove, in the end, to have sounded the death-knell of that nation, it would be" what? ("It would be an act of divine justice richly deserved." *The Open Sore of a Continent,* p. 145.)

XXVII. Climate of Fear: The Quest for Dignity in a Dehumanized World

946. "During the question-and-answer session, I offered the view that the president of the United States had deliberately exaggerated suspicions of the existence of weapons of mass destruction in Iraq. By contrast, I cautioned" what? ("it was impossible, and dangerous, for him or anyone else to underestimate the menace posed to the world by al-Qaeda." *Climate of Fear,* p. vii.)

947. "The last century, post-Second World War, was indeed dominated by" what? ("By the fear of nuclear holocaust. That fear, let it be noted, however, was only a successor to another it replaced, once the war was over—that of world domination by a fanatic individual who preached, and sought to actualize, a gospel of race purity." *Climate of Fear,* p. 11.)

948. "From Niger to Manhattan, the trail of fear had stretched and broadened to engulf the globe, warning its inhabitants that there were" what? ("No longer any categories of the involved or noninvolved. No longer could not just innocents, but even a community of historic victims who inhabit the African continent, lay claim to a protective immunity." *Climate of Fear,* p. 26.)

949. "Certainly, during the entire Vietnam wars, it would have been an excessive claim to suggest" what? ("That the world was trapped in a climate of fear." *Climate of Fear,* p. 41.)

950. "So now, directly to that conundrum— power—just what is that? We know what it does. For

a start, power takes away the freedom of the other and" what? ("And replaces it with fear." *Climate of Fear,* p. 55.)

951.   "And now we come to the nurturing environment of the mantra. As I began my lecture tour of some European universities during that exile, it did not take long for me to realize" what? ("That the mood of the historic Paris uprising was still in the ascendant, never mind the failure of that movement—and perhaps the zeal, being all that was left, was even more willfully embraced on that account." *Climate of Fear,* p. 69.)

952.   "It is not my intention here to pursue the rights and wrongs of the province of the imagination, certainly not my intention to" what? ("To berate or defend a writer accused of disrespect or insensitivity toward religious belief. My concern today is simply to call attention to the contrasting activities of that country, Iran, in a truly elevating mission to restore dialogue to its rightful place as an agent of civilizations." *Climate of Fear,* p. 83.)

953.   "Regarding this context of relationship, however, one common. Reductionism that also courts dismissal is" what" ("Is that of conduct under suffering. Superficially, acceptance or resignation may appear to convey dignified bearing." *Climate of Fear,* p. 97.)

954.   "The quasi-state, we know, sometimes overlaps or interlocks with Community and seeks to take it over. Critical mass occurs at the point at which" when? ("One can no longer be distinguished from the other, and the overrun Community is seen

to appear to bow totally to the control of the quasi-state, if only for a measure of preservation of its own identity." *Climate of Fear,* p. 111.)

955.   "At state is tolerance, and the place of dissent in social interaction. We would do well, however, to note—for practical ends—the differences between" what? ("Between the working of secular intolerance and those of the theocratic order. Such differences may assist us in assessing the very real threat to human freedom that the closed world of fanaticism poses to humanity." *Climate of Fear,* p. 125.)

XXVIII.   Of Africa

956.   "What does the continent known as Africa possess that the rest—or a greater part—of the globe does not have already in superabundance? These, obviously, cannot be limited to material or inert possessions—such as mineral resources, touristic landscapes, strategic locations—not forgetting the continent's centuries-old designation as hatcheries for the supply of cheap labor to other societies, East and West. There also exist" what? ("Dynamic possessions—ways of perceiving, responding, adapting, or simply doing that vary from people to people, including structures of human relationships." *Of Africa,* p. vii.)

957.   "Now, when such questions are posed, there is a tendency to suggest that one is already implying one answer, and one answer only—the disintegration of the present national entities, accompanied or unaccompanied by" what? ("By a reversion to the precolonial conditions of the rudimentary state." *Of Africa,* p. 11.)

958.   "The predominant pattern, alas, has been the temptation to" what? ("To take the easy way out, especially if there are motives that interpose themselves between us and a direct, truthful apprehension of the novelty. For instance, let us say that the aliens we have just encountered on that distant planet possessed mineral resources that we badly covet for our internal development, maybe even for further space exploration. Or perhaps the newly discovered environment is so congenial to humans that we immediately think of expropriating it for settling our excess or idle population,

converting it into an offshore plantation or tourist retreat." *Of Africa,* p. 31.)

959.   "For a long time after independence, Kenya was indeed one such simmering pot of discontent that would finally boil over in 2009. From the Nigerian political class, the nation was" what? ("Was once openly instructed on the divine appropriateness of such a hegemonic theology by an apologist of feudal control." *Of Africa,* p. 51.)

960.   "Haiti remains the first black republic of the modern world, founded and governed by descendants of slaves and thus" what? ("The symbol of revolt against human enslavement throughout the New World, and a beacon for the spirit of freedom anywhere." *Of Africa,* p. 71.)

961.   "As if the continent did not have enough on her plate, enter a shadowy but lethal force determined to" what? ("Determined to reenslave a continent with its chains of fundamentalist theology!" *Of Africa,* p. 93.)

962.   "The Babalawo's clinic intrigued me far more than the starched, white-overall western clinics, where a most impressive looking doctor hung a stethoscope around his neck, listened to heartbeats, took pulses, and wrote down prescriptions in indecipherable script." Why? ("He looked intimidatingly omniscient, and he clearly was in touch with all the dialects of the human body. The Babalawo also exuded knowledge and mystery, but somehow he appeared closer to his patients." *Of Africa,* p. 113.)

963.   "Those very seductions that are the outward embellishments of religions are also" what? ("Are also recognizable as competitive attributes of the secular world, especially those that are" what? ("Those that are raised to ideological ascendancies. The monumental achievements of either fascism or communism, the choreographed, splendor and pageantry that trumpeted their existence, the arts, architecture, and ideological treatises still impress or repel us." *Of Africa,* p. 133.)

964.   "Yorube spiritual accommodativeness, we continue to remind ourselves, is not" what? ("Is not unique to that part of the African world. The following, for instance, comes from the adventures of a South African individual in his search of a spiritual anchor, a search that was as much conditioned by political events as by an innate Orisa temperament, sanctified by the examples laid out in the very histories of the deities' own search for wisdom." *Of Africa,* p. 153.)

965.   "Cultural relativism or respect is therefore not the talismanic mantra for the resolution of the human predicament—indeed, it is only the beginning of" what? ("Of a complete, ethically rigorous exercise, not its terminus. It is especially demanding because it requires a readiness for the interrogation of absolutes—not merely for the culture under scrutiny but for the scrutinizing side which even without so declaring, has already positioned itself on legitimate critical grounds, often presumed higher." *Of Africa,* p. 177.)

Bibliography

Jeyifo, Biodun. 2004. *Wole Soyinka.* Cambridge: Cambridge University Press.

Soyinka, Wole. 1989. *Ake': The Years of Childhood.* New York: Vintage International.

Soyinka, Wole. 1995. *The Beatification of Area Boy, A Lagosian Kaleidoscope.* Auckland: Methuen Drama.

Soyinka, Wole. 1999. *The Burden of Memory, The Muse of Forgiveness.* New York: Oxford University Press.

Soyinka, Wole. 2004. *Climate of Fear, the Quest for Dignity in a Dehumanized World.* New York: Random House.

Soyinka, Wole. 1973. *Collected Plays 1: A Dance of the Forests, The Swamp Dwellers, The Strong Breed, The Road, The Bacchae of Euripides.* New York: Oxford University Press.

Soyinka, Wole. 1974. *Collected Plays 2: The Lion and the Jewel, Kongi's Harvest, The Trials of Brother Jero, Jero's Metamorphosis, Madmen and Specialists.* New York: Oxford University Press.

Soyinka, Wole. 1975. *Death and the King's Horseman.* New York: W.W. Norton, Inc.

Soyinka, Wole. 1994. *Ibadan, the Penkelemes Years a Memoir, 1946-1965.* Auckland: Methuen Drama.

Soyinka, Wole. 1967. *Idanre & Other Poems.* New York: Hill and Wang.

Soyinka, Wole. 1965. *The Interpreters*. London: Andre Deutsch.

Soyinka, Wole. 2015. *Interventions, Between Defective Memory and the Public Lie, A Personal Odyssey in the Republic of Liars*. Ibadan, Nigeria.

Soyinka, Wole. 1991. *Isara, A Voyage Around Essay*. Methuen, MA: Methuen.

Soyinka, Wole. 1972. *The Man Died*. New York: Harper and Row.

Soyinka, Wole. 1988. *Mandela's Earth and Other Poems*. New York: Random House.

Soyinka, Wole. 1977. *Myth, Literature and the African World*. New York: Cambridge University Press.

Soyinka, Wole. 2012. *Of Africa*. London: Yale University Press.

Soyinka, Wole. 1994. *The Open Core of a Continent*. Oxford: Oxford University Press.

Soyinka, Wole. 2004. *Politics, Poetics and Postcolonialism*. Cambridge: Cambridge University Press.

Soyinka, Wole. 2002. *Samarkland, and Other Markets I Have Known*. Methuen, MA: Methuen.

Soyinka, Wole. *Season of Anomy*. Guernsey, UK: Guernsey Press Co.

Soyinka, Wole. 2006. *You Must Set Forth at Dawn, A Memoir*. New York: Random House.

Printed by Amazon Italia Logistica S.r.l.
Torrazza Piemonte (TO), Italy

54268764R00120